Mohamed Issa

# Sequence Analysis Algorithms for Bioinformatics Application

GRIN Verlag

**Bibliografische Information der Deutschen Nationalbibliothek:**

Die Deutsche Bibliothek verzeichnet diese Publikation in der Deutschen National-bibliografie; detaillierte bibliografische Daten sind im Internet über http://dnb.d-nb.de/ abrufbar.

Dieses Werk sowie alle darin enthaltenen einzelnen Beiträge und Abbildungen sind urheberrechtlich geschützt. Jede Verwertung, die nicht ausdrücklich vom Urheberrechtsschutz zugelassen ist, bedarf der vorherigen Zustimmung des Verlages. Das gilt insbesondere für Vervielfältigungen, Bearbeitungen, Übersetzungen, Mikroverfilmungen, Auswertungen durch Datenbanken und für die Einspeicherung und Verarbeitung in elektronische Systeme. Alle Rechte, auch die des auszugsweisen Nachdrucks, der fotomechanischen Wiedergabe (einschließlich Mikrokopie) sowie der Auswertung durch Datenbanken oder ähnliche Einrichtungen, vorbehalten.

**Imprint:**

Copyright © 2014 GRIN Verlag GmbH
Druck und Bindung: Books on Demand GmbH, Norderstedt Germany
ISBN: 978-3-656-74787-1

**This book at GRIN:**

http://www.grin.com/en/e-book/280808/sequence-analysis-algorithms-for-bioinformatics-application

**GRIN - Your knowledge has value**

Der GRIN Verlag publiziert seit 1998 wissenschaftliche Arbeiten von Studenten, Hochschullehrern und anderen Akademikern als eBook und gedrucktes Buch. Die Verlagswebsite www.grin.com ist die ideale Plattform zur Veröffentlichung von Hausarbeiten, Abschlussarbeiten, wissenschaftlichen Aufsätzen, Dissertationen und Fachbüchern.

**Visit us on the internet:**

http://www.grin.com/

http://www.facebook.com/grincom

http://www.twitter.com/grin_com

Zagazig University
Faculty of Engineering
Computers and Systems Engineering Department

# Sequence Analysis Algorithms for Bioinformatics Applications

By

## Mohamed Al sayed Mohamed Ali Issa

B.Sc in Computers and Systems Department, faculty of
Engineering, Zagazig University,
Egypt .

A Thesis submitted to

Faculty of Engineering, Zagazig University

in Partial Fulfillment of the Requirements for

**The Degree of M.Sc.**

In

COMPUTERS AND SYSTEMS ENGINEERING

Faculty of Engineering , Zagazig University, Egypt

**2013**

# Acknowledgments

I would like to thank all of Prof. Ibrahim Ziedan, Prof. Ahmed Al zohairy and Dr.Hitham Abo bakr, for their great efforts during their supervision on the thesis.

Great thanks to Nvidia company for supporting us with two powerful GPU units to perform this work.

Not forget to mention my colleague Eng. Ahmed Al Mansi, for his support in proposing web interface tools.

Last but not least, I would like to acknowledge and extend my heartfelt gratitude to my family for their support and encouragement which has made the completion of this dissertation possible.

# Preface

The common theme of this dissertation is proposing an algorithm that extracting the most nearest two sequences ( ancestors ) to a query sequence (offspring ) with scanning biological database using GPU. Also it determines parts of similarity and difference between the 3 sequences and percentage of similarities. This algorithm called Gene Tracer with scanning database using GPU (GT-DB-GPU ). The material is organized in five chapters. Most of the material has been published in international journal and Jhon Wiley publisher.

Some of the material in Chapter two are published as chapter entitled as "Accelerating Pairwise Alignment Algorithms by Using Graphics Processor Units " in a book entitled as "Biological Knowledge Discovery Handbook: Preprocessing, Mining and Post processing of Biological Data " [M.Issa , Wiley , 2012].

Some of the material in Chapter Three "Gene Tracer algorithm" is proposed and published in IJCA as "Gene-Tracer: Algorithm Tracing Genes Modification from Ancestors through Offsprings " [M.Issa , Vol 52 , No 19 ,2012].

Thesis's works were included in a scientific project from H3ABIONET [http://www.h3abionet.org].

# Abstract

In bioinformatics, it is very important to relate common matched parts between DNA or Protein sequences. Gene Tracer algorithm was proposed to perform this function. Gene Tracer based mainly on local sequence alignment. Local alignment determines the common parts between sequences. Gene Tracer extends this function, so it has three sequences as inputs. It determines common parts between one of the sequences and each one of the other two sequences. Then it locates common substrings in each sequence ( The two ancestors and offspring ). Another important application is determining ancestors sequences of an offspring before it is used in any process. Gene Tracer was extended to scan a large biological database to get the nearest two sequences to offspring sequence. Due to database was large, this application was implemented on Graphical Processing Unit "GPU" to decrease execution time of algorithm. GPU computes alignment for all sequences in database with query in parallel. But CPU executes alignment for all sequences serially. So GPU gives significant reduction of application's execution time than CPU. Execution time also was decreased by increasing occupancy of GPU. Occupancy of GPU means keeping GPU's resources as busy as possible.

There are 3 contributions for this research work. i) Gene Tracer algorithm was proposed to relate DNA or Protein sequences. ii) Gene Tracer with scanning database using GPU algorithm was proposed to search for offspring's ancestors. iii) Effect of GPU's occupancy on execution time was discussed, where execution time of an application was decreased by increasing occupancy.

Keywords : Bioinformatics, Gene Tracer algorithm, GPU.

# Table of Contents

III

# List of Figures

# List of Tables

# List of Abbreviation

| DNA | Deoxyribo- Nucleic Acid |
|---|---|
| RNA | Ribo Nucleic Acid |
| DP | Dynamic programming |
| SW | Smith   Waterman |
| GPU | Graphical Processing Unit |
| GT-DB-GPU | Gene Tracer by scanning database on GPU |
| GT-DB-CPU | Gene Tracer by scanning database on CPU |

# Chapter 1: Introduction

*In this chapter, we give an overview of Bioinformatics with special high light to pairwise sequence alignment. The motivation of our research is presented next. Main objectives and research challenges are then manifested. Main contributions are introduced and the rest of the thesis is finally outlined.*

## 1.1    Bioinformatics

Bioinformatics is a mixture field of biological and information sciences, which study methods of storing, retrieving and analyzing biological data. Biological data include nucleic acid (Deoxy ribonucleic acid "DNA" or Ribonucleic acid "RNA") sequence and protein sequence. This analysis may require the use of different techniques such as algorithms, databases, data mining, web technologies, image processing, modeling and simulation, software engineering, artificial intelligence and statistics. Bioinformatics is useful in many fields such as drug design and genetic engineering.

## 1.2    Bioinformatics cycle

Bioinformatics cycle consists of three stages as shown in figure 1.1. In the first stage, biological data, which represent informations, are extracted from biological experiments in life science. In the second stage biological data are stored in biological database. In the third stage several operations may be performed on biological sequences that retrieved from database such as statistical analysis, visualization, prediction and modeling using information science techniques. The ultimate goal of statistical bioinformatics is to statistically identify significant changes in biological processes for the purpose of answering biological questions. For example if the biologist want to determine originality of biological sequence that was extracted from biological experiments. Analysis tools are used to compare this sequence with sequences in biological databases to determine the most nearest matching sequence for biologist.

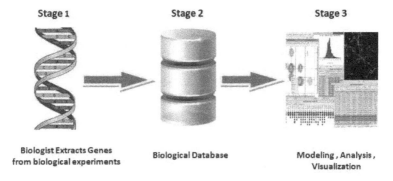

| Stage 1 | Stage 2 | Stage 3 |
| --- | --- | --- |

Biologist Extracts Genes from biological experiments    Biological Database    Modeling, Analysis, Visualization

Figure 1.1 Bioinformatics cycle

## 1.3    A recap of molecular biology

In the following a short recapitulation of the basics of molecular biology is mentioned.

### 1.3.1    DNA

DNA is the basis of inheritance. It is a polymer consisting of small molecules called nucleotides which include four bases adenine (A), cytosine (C), guanine (G) and thymine (T). A DNA sequence is a series of the four alphabets {A, C, G, T}. DNA occurs in double complementary strands where   there is a hydrogen bond between

A & T also a hydrogen bond between  G & C.  Two  strands  of DNA forms a double helix as shown in figure 1.2 [1].

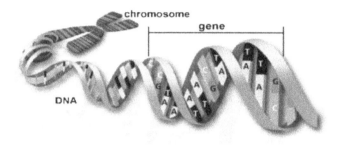

Figure 1.2 Double stands of DNA forms as double helix [1].

### 1.3.2    RNA and transcription

Genetic  informations  are  carried  by  DNA.  Informations  in  DNA  are copied to new copies called mRNA (messenger RNA) and this process is called transcription. The DNA nucleotides A,C,G,T are respectively transcribed into mRNA nucleotides U (uracil (U) replaces thymine (T) in RNA molecules),G,C,A. After transcription to mRNA a translation process to protein occurs as shown in figure1.3.

### 1.3.3    Proteins

Proteins are polypeptide chains, which consist of 20 different alphabet of amino acids. Three mRNA nucleotides encode one of 20 amino acids [1].

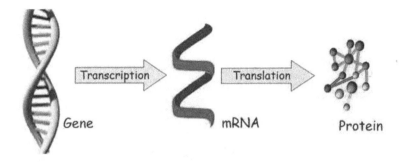

Figure 1.3 Translation from Gene To DNA [1]

## 1.4    Sequence analysis

DNA or protein sequence analysis is a basic research area of bioinformatics. Sequence analysis means analyzing DNA, RNA and proteins sequences using many analytical methods for understanding their features, functions and structures. Sequence alignment or sequence comparison is a public methodology for performing sequence analysis process [2-3].

## 1.5    Sequence alignment

Sequence alignment is the mainly important problem in computational biology. It is used to determine which parts in sequences are a like and which ones are differ [4]. Also it is used to measure the grade of similarity between two or more sequences which gives conclusion about the homology between them [5]. Sequence alignment between two sequences called pairwise alignment and that between more than two sequences is called multiple alignment [6].

In this research work pairwise sequence alignment is focused. Protein or DNA sequences with unknown originality or functionality are often compared with other known sequences stored in large scale biological database (size ~ 300,000 sequence ) to determine their originality or functionality through their alignment. Determining the origin of a sequence is depending on extracting the most nearest matching sequence that has the highest alignment score from biological database [7].

### 1.5.1    Pairwise sequence alignment

Pairwise sequence alignment can be done by hand for very short sequences, so alignment of lengthy, highly variable or extremely numerous sequences cannot be done by human efforts.

In fact there are many alignment algorithms such as dynamic programming ( DP ) that produce high quality sequence alignment. Generally there are three kinds of DP sequence alignment, 1) the local sequence alignment developed by smith – waterman (SW) [8], 2) the global alignment developed by Needleman [9] and 3) semi global alignment [10].

The suitable kind of DP sequence alignment algorithms for searching database is the local sequence alignment. It extracts the most nearest matching sequence that has the longest substring matching between query sequence and each sequence in a database. This algorithm is slow, It consumes many hours to search for sequence about 1024 base and this is impractical for use by biologists but  it has higher accuracy of alignment. Other algorithms based on heuristic methods which is fast were designed for searching large scale biological  database, but it consumes many minutes (30 minute for sequence length about 1024 ) [11] and don't guarantee accurate alignment result.

So DP sequence alignment is suitable for such problem due to it's high accuracy. Scanning biological database time increases due to the rapid growth of it. A speed up technique for this algorithm is proposed in parallel manner using Graphical Processing Unit (GPU) to decrease execution time of alignment algorithms as possible.

## 1.6    Motivations

Pairwise sequence alignment is one of the main bioinformatics applications. As mentioned in section 1.5, its main usage to get the alignment between two sequences. This alignment may be used to get the similarity between the two sequences as global alignment or originality of a sequence as local alignment or used in DNA fragment assembly as semi - global alignment.

We concentrate on pairwise local alignment that used to get originality for a sequence by determining the alignment of common  longest nearest substrings between two sequences. Also is used to extract the nearest sequence from biological database for a query sequence depending on the maximum score of alignment's scores between this query sequence and each sequence in database. This alignment scores not express the length of common substring. Also this algorithm extract alignment of common parts only but not locates it in each sequence.

Another important application is that many biologists need  to find the relation between offspring sequences and two ancestors and also estimation percentage of contribution of each ancestor in offspring sequence or called similarity percentage. Such application cannot be computed by local alignment.

## 1.7    Objectives

This thesis concentrates on developing  pairwise local alignment algorithm so that besides finding the  common substrings between two sequences, it positions these substrings in each sequence. Also developing local alignment to perform function of finding the relations between an offspring sequence and two ancestors.

## 1.8    Main contributions

In the following main contributions in this thesis:

1- Developing pairwise local alignment so that it performs function of finding the relations between offspring sequences and two ancestors sequences and positioning the common parts in each sequence and also estimation of similarity percentage between offspring and each ancestors. This developed algorithm was called Gene Tracer.

2- Another development for Gene Tracer algorithm is instead input two ancestors sequences and  offspring one, it extracts the nearest two sequences from biological databases that matching the maximum length of common parts for an offspring sequence. Then positions common parts in each sequence and computes similarity percentage.

3- For more development for Gene Tracer algorithm is implementing  and executing it on Graphical Processing Unit " GPU " to decrease execution time as much as possible.

4- Study effect of the number of threads per block on GPU's occupancy which affect on GPU's execution time.

The rest of thesis are organized as follows :

**Chapter 2 : Literature review**

This chapter survey previous methods of pairwise sequence alignment and  developments for accelerating it.

**Chapter 3 : Gene Tracer**

This chapter discuss gene tracer algorithm that was proposed to get relations and positions of similarity between three sequences (two ancestor and offspring sequence).

**Chapter 4 : Gene Tracer by scanning database on GPU (GT-DB-GPU) algorithm .**

This chapter discuss proposed algorithm to get the most nearest two sequences to a biological sequence on CPU and GPU, and compare execution time on CPU vs GPU. Also in this chapter more development to accelerate algorithm execution on GPU by discussing effect of GPU's occupancy.

**Chapter 5 : Conclusion and Future work**

This chapter concludes thesis works and suggestion of future work.

# Chapter 2:  Literature Review

*In this chapter; an introduction to pairwise sequence alignment algorithms and it's main applications are presented. Also developments of local alignment algorithms are focused. Then an introduction to GPU and developments of pairwise local alignment using it are presented.*

Sequence alignment used to determine portions of similarity and difference in two sequences. As shown in figure 2.1 two sequences are aligned where similar portions are aligned and different portions are aligned with gap ( – ). There are two main kinds of sequence alignment. The alignment between two sequences called pairwise alignment and alignment between more than two sequences called multiple alignment. In this research, pairwise alignment is focused.

```
S E Q 1   _ A C G G C C A C G G
S E Q 2   G A C C G _ _ A C _ _
```

Figure 2.1 pairwsie sequence alignment.

## 2.1    Pairwise sequence alignment algorithms

There are two approaches for implementing pairwise alignment, a) DP methods which consumes long time of execution but gives highly accurate alignment, b) heuristic methods which may have small execution time but don't gurantee accurate alignment.

## 2.1.1 Dynamic programming pairwise sequence alignment

## algorithms

Dynamic programming is a programming approach like the divide-and-conquer approach ,where the problem is solved by divides it to sub problems and the optimal solution may be obtained [12].

There are three types of DP pairwise sequence alignment a) global sequence alignment, b) local sequence alignment and c) semi-global alignment.

### 1.Global Alignment

A *pairwise global Alignment* involves the alignment of the entire of two sequences. An example of global alignment, the following two sequences GTTCGTTG , GTTCTTG seem to be similar but there is extra nucleotide in the first sequence. So global alignment is used to determine position of similar and different portions in two sequences as follow:

| G | T | T | C | G | T | T | G |
|---|---|---|---|---|---|---|---|
| G | T | T | C | — | T | T | G |

The indel or gap ( — ) in the lower sequence means that there is an extra nucleotide in upper sequence. A DP algorithm called Needleman and Wunsch [13] was proposed for pairwise global alignment. A way for aligning two sequences $S_1$ and $S_2$, with respective lengths $m$ and $n$ using pairwise global alignment may be performed as follow:

(i)A Scoring matrix M of size (m+1)*(n+1) is constructed and initialized using a *substitution matrix*, such as PAM (*Percent Accepted Mutations*) [13], BLOSUM (*BLOcks SUbstitution Matrix*) [14]. Line by line scores are added starting from the left upper cell to the right lower cell where the following equation is used [15 ]:

$$M[i,j] = \max \begin{cases} se(i,j) + M[i-1,j-1], \\ M[i-1,j] + p, \\ M[i,j-1] + p \end{cases}$$  (1)

where $P$ is a gap penalty, $se$ is the score between the character at position $i$ in $S_1$ and the one at position $j$ in $S_2$.

(ii)   Backtrace the scoring matrix by building a path was called maximum score path such as in figure 2.2, which gives an optimal pairwise alignment, such path starts from the lowest right cell to the upper left cell and three types of possible movements are allowed:

   (a) *Diagonal movement*: This movement corresponds to the passage from a cell $(i,j)$ to a cell $(i-1,j-1)$.

   (b) *Vertical movement*: This movement corresponds to the passage from a cell $(i,j)$ to a cell $(i-1,j)$.

   (c) *Horizontal movement*: This movement corresponds to the passage from a cell $(i,j)$ to a cell $(i,j-1)$.

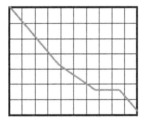

Figure 2.2 Backtracking scoring matrix

## A) Global sequence alignment algorithm

*Needleman_wunch Alignment algorithm with constant gap*
*Input :*

| | |
|---|---|
| $Q\_seq$ : | *sequence // $1^{st}$ sequence* |
| $D\_seq$ : | *sequence // $2^{nd}$ sequence* |
| $M$ : | *length of $Q\_seq$* |
| $N$ : | *length of $D\_seq$* |
| $g$ : | *constant gap cost* |
| $Mat$ : | *match score* |
| $NMat$ : | *mismatch score* |

*Output :*

| | |
|---|---|
| $Q\_seq\_Align$ : | *sequence // $Q\_seq$ Aligned* |
| $D\_seq\_Align$ : | *sequence // $D\_seq$ Aligned* |

*Variable :*

| | |
|---|---|
| *north :* | *contain value of upper cell of current cell* |
| *north_west :* | *contain value of upper left cell of current cell* |
| *west :* | *contain value of left cell of current cell* |
| *H :* | *score matrix length of $(M+1)(N+1)$* |

*Begin*
*// Forward Trace :*

*Sub_mat ($Q\_seq[i]$ , $D\_seq[j]$  )*
*{*
*If( $Q\_seq[i] == D\_seq[j]$  ) return Mat*
*If ( $Q\_seq[i] != D\_seq[j]$  ) return NMat*
*}*
*for i := 0 to M do H 0,i := −i\*g  end*
*for j := 1 to N do H j,0 := −j\*g  end*
*for i := 1 to M do*
  *for j := 1 to N do*
    *north =H[i−1,j] − g*
    *west = H[i,j−1] − g*
    *north_west = H[i−1,j-1]+ Sub_mat ( $Q\_seq[i]$,$D\_seq[i]$)*
     *H[i,j] := max (north ,west,nort_west)*
  *end*
 *end*
*// Backward Trace :*

  *i=(M+1) , j= (N+1) // Start from the lowest right cell.*

  *k=0*

*Align ((M+1),(N+1),k) {*

   *If ( i=0 , j=0 )*

   *Return*

   *If (H[i−1,j] − g = H[i,j])*

   *{*

   *Q_seq_Align[k]=Q_seq[i] , D_seq_Align[k]='_'*

   *k++, Align (i-1,j,k)*

   *}*

*If (H[i,j-1] − g = H[i,j])*

   *{*

   *Q_seq_Align[k]='_' ,D_seq_Align[k]=D_seq[i]*

   *k++, Align (i,j-1,k)*

   *}*

   *If (H[i-1,j-1]+score(Q_seq[i],D_seq[i]) = H[i,j])*

   *{*

   *Q_seq_Align[k]=Q_seq[i] ,D_seq_Align[k]=D_seq[i]*

   *k++,Align (i-1,j-1,k)*

   *}*

      *}*

   *Reverse Q_seq_Align , D_seq_Align*

   *Return  Q_seq_Align , D_seq_Align*

***End***

Time complexity of the algorithm of Needleman and Wunsch is $O(m*n)$ and space complexity is $O(m*n)$ where m, n are lengths of the two sequences.

### B ) Example of global alignment

     Input :    Q_seq= ATAT   ,    D_seq = TATA

For Match score = 1 , Mismatch = -1 , Constant gap penality = 1

Scoring matrix ( H ) :

|   |   | T | A | T | A |
|---|---|---|---|---|---|
|   | **0** | **-1** | -2 | -3 | -4 |
| A | -1 | -1 | **0** | -1 | 2 |
| T | -2 | 0 | -1 | **1** | 0 |
| A | -3 | -1 | 1 | 0 | **2** |
| T | -4 | -2 | 0 | 2 | **1** |

The bold cells are the optimal alignment path starting from the lower right cell and ending at the upper left cell. The first row and column are not included in matrix but to clarify the algorithm.

Output :    Q_seq_Align =    T    A    T    A    –

D_seq_Align=    –    A    T    A    T

Application of global alignment is comparing two genes with almost the same function, for example comparing human's gene versus mouse's gene [17].

**2.Local Alignment :**

A pairwise local Alignment involves the alignment of portions of two sequence as shown in figure 2.3 but global alignment aligning the entire of two sequences. A DP algorithm SW alignment algorithm [8] was proposed for pairwise local alignment .

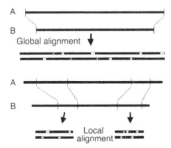

Figure 2.3 Global alignment vs Local alignment

The equation used for calculation of the scoring matrix is as follows[2]:

$$M[i,j] = \max \begin{cases} se(i,j) + M[i-1,j-1], \\ M[i-1,j] + p, \\ M[i,j-1] + p, \\ 0 \end{cases} \qquad (2)\backslash$$

Where M is scoring matrix, $S_1$ is sequence 1 and $S_2$ is sequence 2, $se$ is the score between the character at position $i$ in $S_1$ and the one at position $j$ in $S_2$ and $P$ is a constant gap penalty. With $m$ and $n$ respectively being the lengths of the sequences $S_1$ and $S_2$ [2].

Global alignment differs than local alignment in two points. 1) In local alignment any cell of scoring alignment matrix has minimum score zero, but in global alignment score may be lower than zero. 2) In local alignment backtrace start from cell has maximum score and stop at first cell has score zero, but in global alignment back trace start from lower right cell and end at upper left cell in scoring matrix.

## A ) Local sequence alignment algorithm

Local Alignment algorithm with constant gap

*Input :*

$Q\_seq$ :        *sequence // $1^{st}$ sequence*

$D\_seq$ :        *sequence // $2^{nd}$ sequence*

$M$     :     *length of $Q\_seq$*
$N$     :     *length of $D\_seq$*
$g$     :          *constant gap cost*
*Mat*    :          *match score*
*NMat* :               *mismatch score*
*Output :*
$Q\_seq\_Align$  : *sequence // longest common substring between     $Q\_seq$ ,*

        $D\_seq$

$D\_seq\_Align$ :  *sequence // longest common substring between $Q\_seq$ ,*

        $D\_seq$

*Variable :*
    *north :       contain value of upper cell of current cell*
    *north\_west : contain value of upper left cell of current cell*
    *west :       contain value of left cell of current cell*
    *max\_i\_position : position of maximum value in H matrix in $Q\_seq$*
    *max\_j\_position :   position of maximum value in H matrix in $D\_seq$*
    *H :          score matrix length of $(M+1)(N+1)$*
    *Max\_score:       max score of H matrix*

*Begin*
*// Forward Trace :*

*// the following steps similar to steps of forward trace steps of global
// alignment but differ in max functions compare scores with 0 in local
// alignment .*

*Sub\_mat ($Q\_seq[i]$ , $D\_seq[j]$ )*
    *{*
    *If( $Q\_seq[i]$ == $D\_seq[j]$ ) return Mat*
    *If ( $Q\_seq[l]$ != $D\_seq[j]$ ) return NMat*
    *}*

```
for i := 0 to M do H 0,i := -i*g   end
for j := 1 to N do H j,0 := -j*g   end
 for i := 1 to M do
    for j := 1 to N do
       north =H[i-1,j] - g
       west = H[i,j-1] - g
       north_west = H[i-1,j-1] + Sub_mat ( Q_seq[i],D_seq[i])
          H[i,j] := max (north ,west,nort_west,0)
       end
    end
max_i_position , max_j_position  = Max (H)


// Backward Trace :

k=0 , i=max_i_position, j=max_j_position

Align (i,j,k) {

   If ( H[i,j] = 0 )

          Return

   If (H[i-1,j] - g = H[i,j])

          {

          Q_seq_Align[k]=Q_seq[i] ,D_seq_Align[k]='_'

          k++, Align (i-1,j,k)

          }


   If (H[i,j-1] - g = H[i,j])

          {

          Q_seq_Align[k]='_' ,D_seq_Align[k]=D_seq[i]

          k++, Align (i,j-1,k)

          }


   IF (H[i-1,j-1]+score(Q_seq[i],D_seq[i])  = H[i,j])

          {

          Q_seq_Align[k]=Q_seq[i] ,D_seq_Align[k]=D_seq[i]
```

*k++,Align (i-1,j-1,k)*

*}*

    *}*

*Reverse Q_seq_Align , D_seq_Align*

*Return Q_seq_Align , D_seq_Align*

**End**

Time complexity of the algorithm of Smith and Waterman and also space complexity is $O(m*n)$ [8].

**B ) Example of local alignment**

Input :        Q_seq=GACGG  ,    D_seq = ACGA

For Match score = 1 , Mismatch = -1 , Constant gap penality = 1

Scoring matrix H :

|   |   | G | A | C | G | G |
|---|---|---|---|---|---|---|
|   | 0 | 0 | 0 | 0 | 0 | 0 |
| A | 0 | 0 | 1 | 0 | 0 | 0 |
| C | 0 | 0 | 0 | 2 | 1 | 0 |
| G | 0 | 1 | 0 | 1 | 3 | 2 |
| A | 0 | 0 | 2 | 1 | 2 | 2 |

Starting from the maximum score and ending at first 0 in the optimal alignment path. The maximum score express the length of common substring.

Output :

    Q_seq_Align=        A    C    G

    D_seq_Align=        A    C    G

Application of local alignment is searching for local similarities in large sequences (e.g., newly sequenced genomes) [17].

# 3.Semi – global Alignment

A *pairwise semi-global alignment* [14] is like pairwise global alignment but neglecting *start gaps and end gaps*. Where *start gaps* are gaps that occur before the first character in a sequence ,and end gaps are that occur after the last character in a sequence [4]. An overlap of two sequences is considered an alignment where start and end gaps are ignored.

**A ) Semi - Global  alignment algorithm  with constant gap algorithm**
*// input , output  the same as local and global alignment .*
***Input :***

| | |
|---|---|
| *Q_seq :* | *sequence // $1^{st}$ sequence* |
| *D_seq :* | *sequence // $2^{nd}$ sequence* |
| *M    :* | *length of  Q_seq* |
| *N    :* | *length of  D_seq* |
| *g    :* | *constant gap cost* |
| *Mat    :* | *match score* |
| *NMat :* | *mismatch score* |

***Output :***
| | |
|---|---|
| *Q_seq_Align  :* | *sequence // Q_seq Aligned* |
| *D_seq_Align :* | *sequence // D_seq Aligned* |

***Variable :***
| | |
|---|---|
| *north :* | *contain value of upper cell  of current cell* |
| *north_west :* | *contain value of upper left cell  of current cell* |
| *west :* | *contain value of left  cell  of current cell* |
| *max_i_position :* | *row of   maximum  value in last column of H matrix in D_seq* |
| *H :* | *score matrix length of (M+1)(N+1)* |
| *Max_score:* | *max score of H matrix in last column* |

***Begin***
*// **Forward Trace :***

*Sub_mat (Q_seq[i] , D_seq[j]   )*
  *{*
    *If( Q_seq[i] = = D_seq[j]   ) return  Mat*
    *If ( Q_seq[i] != D_seq[j]   ) return  NMat*
  *}*
*for i := 0 to M do H 0,i := −i\*g   end*
*for j := 1 to N do H j,0 := −j\*g   end*

- 19 -

```
for i := 1 to M do
    for j := 1 to N do
        north =H[i−1,j] − g
        west = H[i,j−1] − g
        north_west =  H[i−1,j-1]+ Sub_mat ( Q_seq[i],D_seq[i])
        H[i,j] := max (north ,west,nort_west)
    esnd
end
max_j_position  = Max (H) // get max score in last column
```

// **Backward Trace :**

```
k=0 , i=max_i_position , j=(N+1)
Align (i,j,k) {
    If ( H[i,j] = 0 )
            Return
    If (H[i−1,j] − g = H[i,j])
            {
            Q_seq_Align[k]=Q_seq[i] ,D_seq_Align[k]='_'
            k++, Align (i-1,j,k)
            }
    If (H[i,j-1] − g = H[i,j])
            {
            Q_seq_Align[k]='_' ,D_seq_Align[k]=D_seq[i]
            k++, Align (i,j-1,k)
            }
    IF (H[i-1,j-1]+score(Q_seq[i],D_seq[i])  = H[i,j])
            {
            Q_seq_Align[k]=Q_seq[i] ,D_seq_Align[k]=D_seq[i]
            k++,Align (i-1,j-1,k)
            }
            }
Reverse Q_seq_Align , D_seq_Align
```

*Return  Q_seq_Align , D_seq_Align*

**End**
Time complexity of Semi – Global alignment algorithm and also space complexity is $O(m*n)$.

**B ) Example of Semi - Global  alignment algorithm**
Input :          Q_seq= CA          ,          D_seq=GACAAG

For Match score = 1 , Mismatch = -1 , Constant gap penality = 1

Scoring matrix : (H)

|   |   | C | A |
|---|---|---|---|
|   | 0 | 0 | 0 |
| G | 0 | -1 | -1 |
| A | 0 | -1 | 0 |
| C | 0 | 1 | 0 |
| A | 0 | 0 | 2 |
| A | 0 | 1 | 1 |
| G | 0 | 0 | 0 |

Output :

Q_seq_Align =     G     A     C     A     A     G

D_seq_Align =     –     –     C     A     –     –

Application of Semi – Global alignment algorithm are DNA assembly fragment [17] .

## 2.2     Accelerating DP pairwise sequence alignment

Time and space complexities of the three kinds of DP pairwise alignment is large and increases as biological sequence length increases. So many efforts were performed to reduce time and space complexties.

Space is often the limiting factor when computing sequence alignment for long biological sequences, many biological literature have proposed space saving strategies like Hirschberg DP   algorithm [18] that   requires only space proportional to the  sum of the  sequence lengths. So the space complexity of sequence alignment algorithm be linear. But the time complexity still quadratic.

For time complexity , many development are proposed to overcome slowely execution of  DP sequence alignment such as heuristic methods . Many heuristic sequence alignment were proposed  that attempting to keep  as much sensitivity as possible but don't guarantee accurate alignment. Such as FASTA [19], BLAST[20] , SSEARCH [21].

FASTA is a heuristic tools proposed by lipman and pearson that find local similar regions between two sequences but faster than dynamic programming approach. Although the FASTA algorithm is faster than  any of the previous algorithms, it is not guaranteed to find the optimal alignment  between the two sequences.

Another development to FASTA algorithm is BLAST (Basic Local Alignment Search Tool) that approximate measure of alignment as DP alignment and similar to FASTA but faster than FASTA. SSEARCH is another heuristic tool that was proposed to accelerate execution time of sequence alignment algorithm faster than FASTA and BLAST.

With the new sequencing technologies, the number of biological sequences  is increasing exponentionally.  In addition, the length of of these sequences is large, hundreds of bases. So alignment between a query sequence and the sequences in biological databases becomes expensive in computing time and memory space.

So other developments like parallel solutions developed for accelerating this process. These parallel techniques such as  using multi core CPU  that reduce complexity of time such as an algorithm was developed and implemented on 8 core multiprocessor [22].

Also there are many hardware accelerators [23] may be used to accelerate sequence alignment algorithm such as General purpose multicore, Field Programmable Gate Arrays "FPGAs" and Graphics Processing Unit "GPU".

Many parallel techniques take the advantage of single instruction multiple data "SIMD". where the same instruction executed on many cores and do the same function but in different data. Such as Farrar [24] compute the SW algorithm using SSE2 SIMD on intel processors. Farrar's algorithm implementation achieve 2-8 speed up than other implementations using SIMD techniques . Farrar's implementation was then optimized by Rognes [25] to further enhancing the performance. Rognes implemented the stripped algorithm on SSE3 and Linux 64 bit.

FPGAs have been used to implement SW in many solutions . Zhang et al. [26] propose a field programmable gate array (FPGA) solution for the SW algorithm. Their solution provides 250 times faster than a CPU version running on a 2.2 GHz Opteron processor.

They presented impressive speedups over software implementations. However, they are still not considered to be commodity hardware and their programming interface is rather complex. Due to the limited storage, FPGAs cannot produce the alignment for huge sequences.

Due to FPGAs are expensive and has limited space storage, GPUs are used to do sequence alignment for huge sequences and with highly speed up than implementation on FPGAs. In the following section GPU's architecture and programming are discussed briefly.

## 2.3 Graphics processing unit ( GPU ):

Graphics processing unit is a device that was designed to accelerate the computation of Graphics operations. GPU is basically an electronic device consisting of many processors with memory. It was used to accelerate image building for output to a display unit. GPU has high memory bandwidth and high computational capabilities and higher parallel structure that makes it useful as a general purpose unit for other applications rather than any imaging applications like computational biology, financial work and many other applications.

A GPU consists of many multiprocessors and a large Dynamic RAM (DRAM). Each multiprocessor is coupled with a small cache memory and consists of a large number of cores, i.e., Arithmetic Logical Units (ALUs), controlled by a control unit.

Comparison between GPU and CPU is as shown in figure 2.4. A CPU consists of a small number of ALUs and a large DRAM and a single large cache memory. GPU has large number of ALUs (Arithmatic Logic Unit) that give it high computational power in performing data parallel computations faster than CPU. GPU has small cache memory and control unit for each set of ALUs. Also GPU has a higher bandwidth between memory and processing elements (ALUs) that make it performing operations faster.

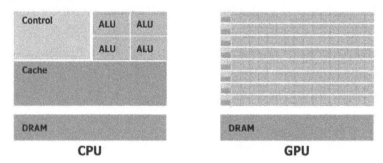

Figure 2.4 CPU organization versus GPU one [27]

As shown in figure 2.5 show memory bandwidth for the CPU vs GPU. For different versions of GPU and CPU memory bandwidth which measured as number of gigabyte per second of GPU is higher than CPU's memory bandwidth.

Figure 2.6 show the evolution of *FLoating-point Operations Per Second* (FLOPS) .Number of floating point per operation in GPUs is higher than that in CPUs. Figures [2.5 , 2.6] show speed and powerful computation speed of GPU over CPU.

GPUs are used in game consoles, embedded systems, mobile phones and computers. In a computer, a GPU can be found on a video card, or on the motherboard. Most of the new desktop and notebook computers have integrated GPUs.

GPUs were originally designed to accelerate computer Graphics algorithms. However, their high computational capabilities and their highly parallel structure opened up to them a wide a range of other fields, like scientific computing [28], computational geometry [29] and bioinformatics [30]. In bioinformatics, mainly GPUs were adopted to accelerate pairwise alignment algorithms.

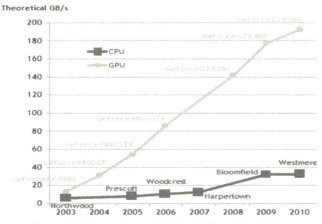

Figure 2.5 Memory bandwidth for CPU and GPU [27]

- 25 -

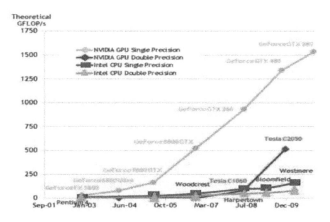

Figure 2.6 FLOPS for CPU and GPU [27]

## 2.3.1   GPU programming model

GPU can be programmed  using OpenGL [31] or  new released library from
Nvidia called  the *Compute Unified Device Architecture* (CUDA) [32]. CUDA
is  a  scalable  parallel  programming  model  and  a  software  environment  for
parallel computing, and also is an extension for C programming language.

A program that can be executed on GPU is  written in C language. It  consists of
two parts serial and parallel.   The serial part  is executed on CPU and the
parallel part is executed on GPU .  The parallel part is written as a function
called kernel which is executed on GPU.

There are two compilers one for C code and the other for GPU code called
NVCC compiler proposed by Nvidia [27].  NVCC output compiled parallel part
to be executed on GPU.    CPU executes serial code and launches  kernel to
GPU  grid to execute the parallel code where grid consists of blocks of thread
that is assigned to kernel as in figure 2.7.

- 26 -

Then CPU execute another serial code till reaches another parallel code and launch another kernel to another GPU grid as in figure 2.8. This manner of execution is called heterogeneous execution.

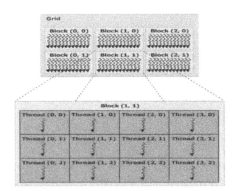

Figure 2.7 programming model for programming on GPU [27]

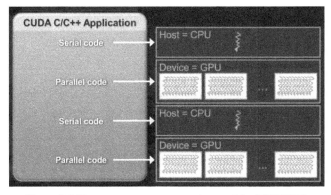

Figure 2.8 Heterogeneous programming model of GPU [27]

## 2.3.2    Threads

Executing parallel program on GPU is performed by launching a kernel on a grid of blocks and each block consist of set of threads. All threads execute the same kernel but on different data.

Threads are grouped in blocks where there is a limit on the number of threads per block. Blocks can be grouped in a grid as shown in figure 2.7 where each grid launches a certain kernel and many grids can do many different functions in parallel. There are many cores on GPU each core executes a thread and many threads are scheduled on this core.

An advantage of these threads of GPU than threads of CPU is that they are light weight meaning that they don't waste time for scheduling or launching a core. Threads can be synchronized at certain break point on a kernel function which means each core reaches a breakpoint of synchronization stalls execution for this thread until all threads reach the same break point.

## 2.3.3   GPU Memory :

GPU memory consists of an on – chip memory with processors like shared , local memory and registers and off chip memory which is separated from processors like global, constant and texture memory. Table 2-1 show difference between GPU memories.

Table 2-1 GPU memories

| Memory | Read / Write access | Speed | Size |
|---|---|---|---|
| Register | Read-write per-thread | Fast | Very limited |
| Local | Read-write per-thread | slow | Limited |
| Shared | Read-write per- block | Fast | Very limited |
| Global | Read-write per- grid | slow | Large |
| Constant | Read-only per-grid | slow | Limited |
| Texture | Read-only per- grid | slow | Large |

There are differnet access time to different memory that is as shown in figure 2.9. This figure show access time to each memory of GPU by processors where global memory has the highest access time around 400 – 600 cycle. Access time for constant cache, texture cache and shared memory approximately is the same as access time to registers 1 cycle.

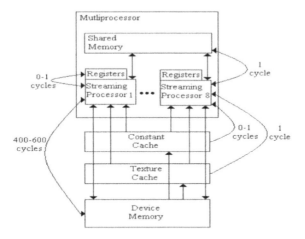

Figure 2.9 Access time between processors and different memory of GPU
device [11, 27]

## 2.4 Accelerating sequence alignment on GPU :

GPUs have a massively parallel architecture. With GPUs impressive
speedups can be achieved using a programming model that is simpler than
the one required for FPGAs. GPU programming is based on OpenGL [31]
and now on CUDA parallel programming languages which is the computing
engine in NVIDIA Graphics processing units [27].

The first implementations of SW algorithm on GPUs are described in [33].
This implementation uses OpenGL. The implementation has two versions, the
first one is with traceback for computing alignment and the second one is
without traceback. Using an Nvidia GeForce 7800 GTX card, their
implementation achieves a 10-fold speedup over SSEARCH .

SW-CUDA [34] is used CUDA for sequence alignment implementation on GPU
. Each GPU thread computes the whole alignment of the query sequence with
one database sequence. The threads are grouped in a *grid* of *blocks* during

execution. In order to make the most efficient use of the GPU resources , the computing time of all the threads in the same *grid* must be as near as possible. Experimental studies have been done to compare SW- CUDA running on two Geforce 8800 GTX with BLAST [20] and SSEARCH [21] , running on a 3 GHz *Intel Pentium IV* processor. The execution times of CUDA implementation were up to 30 times faster than SSEARCH and up to 2.4 times faster than BLAST. SW- CUDA was also 3 times faster than *Single Instruction Multiple Data* (SIMD) implementation [24].

SW – CUDA needed to be improved to utilize the full resources on the GPU because it use local memory of GPU which is the slowest memory resource on GPU.

An effective development [35] is proposed that using on-chip shared memory that reducing amount of data transfer from global memory to processing elements in a GPU. That gives result of reducing data fetch amount to 1 / 140.

An implementation proposed by Striemer [11] is 23 times speed than SSEARCH. SW computation matrix are computed purely using on GPU in Striemer's Implementation. It works in 3 stages, 1) load biological sequences database to GPU's global memory. 2) Each thread used to compute alignment score between a query sequence and each sequence in a database. 3) Alignment scores back to CPU to determine highest alignment score. So this implementation used to give alignment score only not the alignment.

Unlike SW - CUDA, this implementation don't involve using of CPU for partial SW computations, it were done purely using GPU. Another difference that this implementation use constant memory of GPU to save query sequence and substitution matrix because constant cache has access time as register access time as shown in figure 2.9.

Striemer's implementation of SW alignment using GPU has two nested loops as shown in figure 2.10.

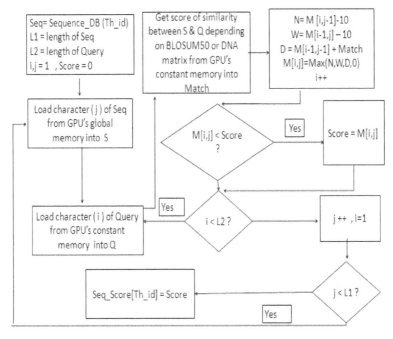

Figure 2.10 Flow chart of G.Striemer implementation on GPU [11].

For each loop of the outer loops character of database sequence is got. Then the inner loops compute alignment scores between this database sequence character and all query sequence characters. Constant memory contain query sequence and BLOSUM50 [14], so accessing constant cache will reduce execution time due to access to constant cache need $0 - 1$ cycle as shown in figure 2.9. Also shared memory used to save temporary calculations of SW computation, this also reduce execution time because access to shared memory need 1 cycle. After computing SW computation matrix for each sequence in database with query sequence using GPU, alignment score for each database sequence saved in global memory of GPU and transfer all scores to CPU to determine the sequence that has the highest alignment score. So this implementation used to compute alignment scores only not the alignment of sequences.

An example of striemer's alignment on GPU is as shown in figure 2.11. It computes alignment score between database sequence has 4 residue (character) and query sequence has 8 residue, where cell calculations matrix used to save temporary alignment scores for each column. Cell calculations matrix used to save temporary alignment score for each column to be used in computing alignment scores of next column. Initially cell calculations matrix is filled with zeros.

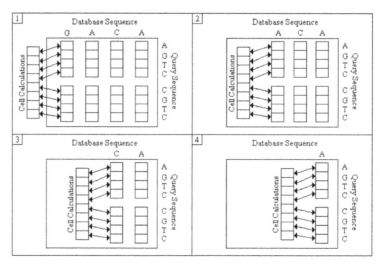

Figure 2.11 An example of aligning query sequence 8 residues and database sequence has 4 residues [11].

Each step in figure as follow: 1) compute alignment scores in column of database sequence character 'G' 4 cell each time and then save this scores in cell calculations matrix. 2) Compute alignment scores between 'A' and query sequence in column 2 using previous scores in cell calculation matrix and then save it in cell calculation matrix. 3) Repeat step 1 & 2 for column 3 and 4 respectively. The largest score in each column is saved. Finally the largest score in all columns represents the alignment score between the two sequence.

## 2.5    Conclusion

In this chapter we listed the most famous available pairwise dynamic programming sequence alignment algorithms that are available and documented. We found that there are three alignment algorithms, 1) global alignment, 2) local alignment, semi-global alignment. This thesis focuses on local alignment algorithm that is used to get similar portions between two sequences. We listed the development for local alignment algorithm in time and space complexity. Developments using hardware accelerator such as multi-core CPU,FPGA and GPU were also mentioned. These hardware accelerators speed execution of local alignment algorithm.

We found that all development algorithms for local alignment algorithms used to get alignment between similar parts in two sequences.

In chapter 3, we proposed an algorithm that was development for local alignment algorithm called Gene Tracer. This algorithm determines longest common substrings between two sequences and is used to determine common portions between offspring sequence and it's ancestors sequences and percentage of similarity.

In chapter 4, we developed Gene Tracer algorithm to extract the nearest two sequences ( ancestors ) to offspring sequence from biological database. GPU was used for speeding up executing of this algorithm and compared to execution of algorithm on CPU.

# Chapter 3:   Gene Tracer algorithm

*In this chapter, we present a proposed algorithm , called Gene Tracer that is used to get relations between sequences to determine homology of them. This algorithm is used in application such as determining originality or functionality of sequences. In other words gene tracer is used to trace genes modification from ancestors sequences through offspring sequence. It tracks down genes modification in the ancestor sequences and finds related parts of each ancestor sequence in the offspring one.*

## 3.1    Overview

*Gene Tracer* can find precisely the location of the ancestor sequences contribution inside the offspring one and gives statistical results that express the relationship between the two ancestor sequences and their offspring one as shown in figure 3.1.

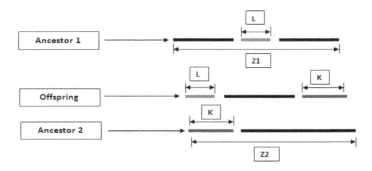

Figure 3.1 : Gene tracer function

Gene Tracer's inputs are two ancestor sequences and one offspring sequence. Gene Tracer's output is as shown in figure 3.1 the output is three sequences have colored parts which represent the matching parts. Longest matching parts common between ancestor 1 and offspring sequence are given a red color with length L and the total length of ancestor 1 is Z1 then matching percentage is L / Z1. The same was done with ancestor 2 and offspring but in blue color and percentage is K / Z2.

## 3.2    Gene tracer algorithm

*Gene Tracer* has three sequences *A_Seq1* (ancestor 1), *A_Seq2* (ancestor 2) and *Off_Seq* (offspring). Gene Tracer operates in two steps, The first step is that it constructs a local alignment [8] between *A_Seq1* and *Off_Seq*. The second step is constructing another local alignment between *A_Seq2* and *Off_Seq*. Based on the constructed alignments, The location of the ancestor sequences contribution inside the offspring one can be found precisely. Statistical results that express the relationships that exist between the two ancestor sequences and the offspring one may be found. A Gene Tracer based on Smith - waterman algorithm [8] is presented in the following section and a complete description of Smith - waterman algorithm was presented in chapter 2.

As stated in chapter 1, Gene Tracer algorithm was modified of SW local alignment algorithm. The modifications are as following:

1- Determining locations of common substrings in both ancestors and offspring sequences.

2- Distinguishing these common substrings by giving them clear and different color.

These modifications are as shown in the following algorithm.

**Gene Tracer** Algorithm

**Inputs**

$A\_Seq1$ : sequence // $1^{st}$ Ancestor sequence

$A\_Seq2$ : sequence // $2^{nd}$ Ancestor sequence

$Off\_Seq$ : sequence // Offspring sequence :

**Outputs**

*Ancestor1* : sequence // *A_Seq1but common parts with Off_Seq in red* colored

*Ancestor2* : sequence // *A_Seq2but common parts with Off_Seq in blue* colored

*Off* : sequence // *Off_Seq but common parts with A_Seq1 & A_Seq2 are*

*//colored in red and blue*

*Percent1, Percent2* : real // Percentages of common parts between ancestors

// and offspring length to an ancestor length (*A_Seq1* or *A_Seq2*)

**Variables**

$L$ : integer // length of common part between Off_Seq & (A_Seq1 or A_Seq2)

$i$ : integer // end position of common part in *A_Seq1* or *A_Seq2*

$j$ : integer // end position of common part in *Off_Seq*

*Match : integer* // score of aligning two identical residues (characters)

*NonMatch : integer* // score of aligning two different residues

*ConstGap : integer* // score of aligning residue with gap.

**Functions:**

*// Local alignment between two sequences A_seq & Off_seq and determines*

*//length and positions of common parts.*

*Smith_Waterman ( A_seq, Off_Seq, Match, NonMatch, ConstGap, L, i, j)*

*{*

*temp_score=0*

for (k=0 ; k< Length (Off_Seq) ) {

    for (z=0;z< Length (A_Seq)){

      *north =H[z−1,z] − ConstGap*

$$west = H[k,k-1] - ConstGap$$

$$if \ (A\_Seq \ [k] == Off\_Seq \ [z])$$
$$\{$$
$$north\_west = H[k-1,z-1] + \ Match$$
$$else$$
$$north\_west = H[k-1,z-1] + \ NonMatch$$
$$\}$$
$$H[k,z] := max \ (north \ , \ west, \ nort\_west, 0)$$

$$SW\_matrix[i][j] = H[k,z]; \ // \ assign \ SW \ computation \ matrix$$
$$\}$$
$$If \ ( \ H > temp\_score \ )$$
$$\{$$
$$temp\_score = H \ ;$$
$$temp\_i = k \ ;$$
$$temp\_j = z \ ;$$
$$\}$$
$$\}$$
$$L = temp\_score$$
$$i = temp\_i$$
$$j = temp\_j$$
$$\}$$

**Begin**

// Step 1 : construct local alignment between *A_Seq1* and *Off_Seq*

*Match = 1*

*NonMatch = 1*

*ConstGap = 1*

*Smith_Waterman (A_Seq1, Off_Seq, Match, NonMatch, ConstGap, L, i, j)*

*Ancestor1:=Color_seq(A_Seq1, i-L, L)*

*Off:=Color_Seq(Off_Seq, j-L, L)*

*Percent1:= L / length(A_Seq1)*

// Step 2 : Construct local alignment between *A_Seq2* and *Off_Seq*

*Smith_Waterman (A_Seq2, Off_Seq, Match, NonMatch, ConstGap, L, i, j)*

*Ancestor2:=Color_seq(A_Seq2, i-L, L)*

*Off :=Color_Seq(Off_Seq, j-L, L)*

*Percent2:= L / length(A_Seq2)*

*Return Ancestor1, Ancestor2, Percent1, Percent2*

**End**

Where : *Smith_Waterman (A_Seq1, Off_Seq, Match, NonMatch, ConstGap, L, i, j)* is the Smith and Waterman algorithm [8] with modifications that it returns length of common substring and its location in each sequence and also distinguish this common substring in clear color in each sequence in stead of return score of alignment or alignment between common substrings only. It receives as input the sequences *A_Seq1, Off_Seq*, the match score *Match*, the non match score *NonMatch* and the constant gap value *ConstGap*. It returns L with maximum score in SW computation matrix which represent length of longest common substring. Also returns positions of end of common substring ( i ) in ancestors sequences (A_seq1 or A_seq2) and ( j ) in offspring sequence. *Color_Seq(A_Seq1, i-L, L)* is a function to color a sequence from position (*i-L*) to position *L*.

*Gene Tracer* algorithm is of complexity $O(max(M,N)*P)$ in computing time and memory space, where *M*, *N* and *P* are respectively the lengths of *A_Seq1*, *A_Seq2* and *Off_Seq* sequences.

## 3.3　Gene Tracer Flow chart

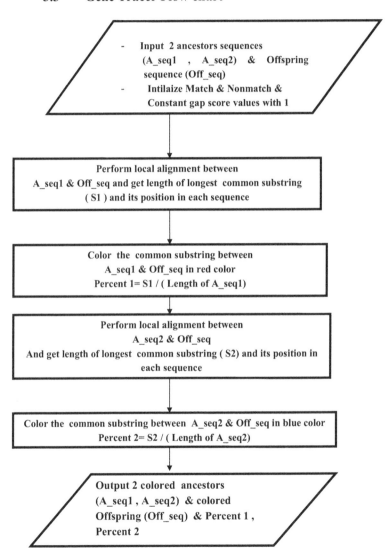

- Input 2 ancestors sequences (A_seq1 , A_seq2) & Offspring sequence (Off_seq)
- Intilaize Match & Nonmatch & Constant gap score values with 1

Perform local alignment between A_seq1 & Off_seq and get length of longest common substring ( S1 ) and its position in each sequence

Color the common substring between A_seq1 & Off_seq in red color Percent 1= S1 / ( Length of A_seq1)

Perform local alignment between A_seq2 & Off_seq And get length of longest common substring ( S2) and its position in each sequence

Color the common substring between A_seq2 & Off_seq in blue color Percent 2= S2 / ( Length of A_seq2)

Output 2 colored ancestors (A_seq1 , A_seq2) & colored Offspring (Off_seq) & Percent 1 , Percent 2

## 3.4    Implementation of Gene Tracer program

The   Gene  Tracer  algorithm  was  implemented  and  coded  in  php  ( web
programming language). It  was  executed  on  a  2.27  GHZ  core  i3  machine
running windows 7 with 4 GB of RAM. In what follow, results of Gene Tracer
program for DNA and Proteins sequences.

### 3.4.1    For DNA :
*Inputs :*

*Ancestor1*: CGCCGGTCGCGGCTGCCCATGCAGG
*Ancestor2*: AGGCAGCGTGTCACGC
*Offspring*: CGCGGCAGGCA

**Ancestor 1 Match Result**

Ancestor

Offspring/Hybrid

Ancestor  C G C C G G T C G C G G C T G C C C A T G C A G G

Offs/Hyb  C G C G G C A G G C A

Match Percentage:  24%

Execution Time:  ~6 Millisecond

**Ancestor 2 Match Result**

Ancestor

Offspring/Hybrid

Ancestor  A G G C A G C G T G T C A C G C

Offs/Hyb  C G C G G C A G G C A

Match Percentage:  31.25%

Execution Time:  ~6 Millisecond

Figure 3.2 : Output of Gene Tracer for DNA sequences

Figure 3.2 shows the obtained results:  In the upper part of this figure, Locations
of common substrings are represented graphically but for real  matched portions

between *ancestro1 sequence* and *offspring* sequence are in red and match percentage between these sequences is also given also execution time is presented. The same for *ancestor2 sequence* and *offspring sequence* in the lower part.

## 3.4.2   For Proteins :

*Inputs :*

*Ancestor 1 :*

AKIKAYNLTVEGVEGFVRYSRVTKQHVAAFLKELRHSKQYENVNLIHYIL

*Ancestor 2: :*

AERYCMRGVKNTAGELVSRVSSDADPAGGWCRKWYSAHRGPDQDAALGSFCIKNP
GAAD

*Offspring :*

AGGWCRKWKQYENVNLIHYI

The output is as shown in figure 3.3 , 3.4

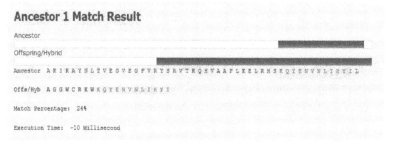

Figure 3.3 : Output of Gene Tracer for proteins (Ancestor1 and offspring sequences)

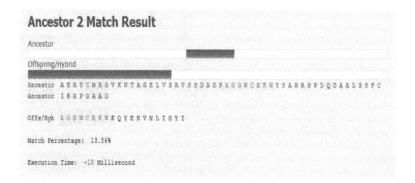

Figure 3.4 : Output of Gene Tracer for proteins (Ancestor 2 and offspring sequences)

## 3.5 Conclusion

In this chapter, Gene Tracer algorithm was presented. It has Three sequences ancestor 1 , ancestor 2 and offspring as input. It output the same input sequences but common substrings between ancestor 1 and offspring is presented in the red color and the same for ancestor 2 and offspring but in blue color. Also it estimates percentage of contribution of ancestors sequences in offspring sequence In the next chapter we will present the extended Gene Tracer algorithm that extracts the nearest two ancestors sequences to offspring sequence from biological database instead of be input for it. Also for more time development for algorithm it will be executed on GPU.

# Chapter 4: Gene Tracer by scanning database on GPU (GT-DB-GPU) algorithm

*Gene Tracer algorithm is used to determine the relationships and positions of common substrings between a certain query sequence (ex. offspring) and two other sequences ( ex. ancestors ). One of the main contributions is that the algorithm is extended to scan a biological database to extract the nearest two ancestors sequences to an offspring sequence based on the longest common substring between offspring sequence and each one of ancestors sequences.*

*Gene Tracer algorithm based on local alignment. Local alignment takes significant execution time on a CPU. Consequently, scanning database by Gene Tracer algorithm is extended to be executed on GPU to minimize execution time as possible because GPU has many cores and executed applications parallel as SIMD (Single Instruction Multiple Data) kind. Where each core execute the same application but on different data (sequences in database).*

*Another development for execution application on GPU was discussing influence of number of threads per block on GPU's occupancy and so on execution time on GPU. Therefore one of main contributions is determining the suitable number of threads per block that give an occupancy 100% and decrease execution time as possible.*

## 4.1 GT-DB-GPU algorithm

GT-DB-GPU algorithm operates in 3 steps. *The first step* is as shown in figure 4.1, i) GT-DB-GPU load sequences from database to GPU memory. The algorithm uses local sequence alignment [8] to extract the nearest 100 sequences to query sequence. ii) Sequence alignment between the query and each sequence in the database is used to determine their relations through a thread of a GPU for each sequence. iii) Alignment scoring matrix is computed for each sequence in the database using BLOSUM50 [36] substitution matrix for proteins is as shown in table 4.1 and table 4.2 for DNA and the constant gap is -10. The highest score in scoring matrix is preserved for each sequence. iv) Alignment scores of all sequences of database with query sequences are returned to the CPU. CPU extracts 100 sequences from database those have the highest 100 score and stores these 100 sequences in a new database called Gene Tracer database.

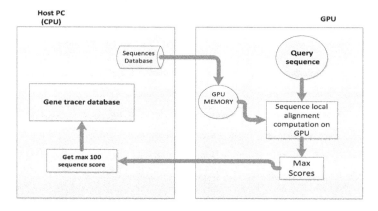

Figure 4.1 The first step of (GT-DB-GPU) algorithm.

Table 4-1 part of BLOSUM 50 substitution matrix .

|   | C | H | W |
|---|---|---|---|
| C | 13 | -3 | -5 |
| H | -3 | 10 | -3 |
| W | -5 | -3 | 15 |

Table 4-2 substitution matrix for DNA .

|   | A | C | G | T |
|---|---|---|---|---|
| A | 10 | -10 | -10 | 5 |
| C | -10 | 10 | 5 | -10 |
| G | -10 | 5 | 10 | -10 |
| T | 5 | -10 | -10 | 10 |

As shown in table 4.2 scoring substitutions matrix has a high score of 10 is given for matched nucleotides (characters). For A with T or G with C the score is 5 because they are in the same biological group. For A with C or G with T the score of -10 is given because they are in different biological group.

*The second step*, The nearest two sequences are extracted from the new database in the same way as in the first step as follow as shown in figure 4.2. i) 100 sequences in new databases are loaded to the GPU. ii) Alignment scores between query sequence and each sequence in gene tracer database is computed but using substitution matrix may be called coincidence matrix. Coincidence matrix for proteins as shown in table 4.3 and table 4.4 for DNA. Where for matched residues in proteins or nucleotides in DNA (residue or nucleotide is each character of sequence), score is 1 and for mismatched residues score is -1. For a constant gap is -1.

These scores are the length of longest common substring between a query sequence and each sequence of 100 sequences in Gene Tracer database .

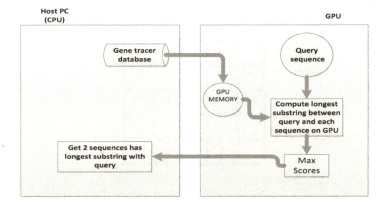

Figure 4.2 The second step of (GT-DB-GPU) algorithm.

Table 4-3 part of coincidence matrix for proteins.

|   | C | H | W |
|---|---|---|---|
| C | 1 | -1 | -1 |
| H | -1 | 1 | -1 |
| W | -1 | -1 | 1 |

Table 4-4 Coincidence matrix for DNA .

|   | A | C | G | T |
|---|---|---|---|---|
| A | 1 | -1 | -1 | -1 |
| C | -1 | 1 | -1 | -1 |
| G | -1 | -1 | 1 | -1 |
| T | -1 | -1 | -1 | 1 |

Coincidence matrix is used for alignment because score of alignment using this matrix is the length of longest common substring. But scores that were computed using BLOSUM50 matrix don't represent the length of longest common substring that is as shown in the following example.

Query = **LMNCCH** , Sequence 1 = **CCPKLM** , Sequence 2 =**LMNPA**

Result of alignment's scores using BLOSUM50 and Coincidence matrices are as shown in table 4.5.

Table 4-5 Differnce between using BLOSUM50 and Coincidence matrices

| | Substitution Matrix | Sequence 1 score | Sequence 2 Score |
|---|---|---|---|
| Query | BLOSUM50 | 26 | 19 |
| | Coincidence | 2 | 3 |

Common substring between query and sequence 1 is : **CC**

Common substring between query and sequence 2 is : **LMN**

As shown in the example, although sequence 1 has higher score than sequence 2 using BLOSUM50 substitution matrix, but sequence 2 has longer common substring with query than sequence 1's common substring with query. So it's clear that local alignment'score using coincidence substitution matrix represent the real length of matched characters between two sequences.

One of main contributions of this thesis is development for local alignment algorithm is to use first BLOSUM50 matrix to compute the alignment between sequences of database and query and extract the best 100 sequences that have the highest alignment scores with query sequence. Then using coincidence matrix to compute the alignment score between the 100 sequences and query sequence. Score using coincidence matrix represents length of common substring between any sequences of 100 and the query sequence. Positions of each score are preserved. Where positions are row and column numbers in each sequence's scoring matrix in the database. Where row number means end of longest common substring in query and column number means end of longest common substring in sequence. as shown in the following.

Scoring matrix for alignment of Query and Sequence 2:

|   |   | L | M | N | P | A |
|---|---|---|---|---|---|---|
|   | 0 | 0 | 0 | 0 | 0 | 0 |
| L | 0 | 1 | 0 | 0 | 0 | 0 |
| M | 0 | 0 | 2 | 1 | 0 | 0 |
| N | 0 | 0 | 1 | 3 | 2 | 1 |
| C | 0 | 0 | 0 | 2 | 2 | 1 |
| C | 0 | 0 | 0 | 1 | 1 | 1 |
| H | 0 | 0 | 0 | 0 | 0 | 0 |

The maximum score in matrix is the length of common parts. The row number is the shaded row from maximum score and represent end of common substring in query. The column number is the shaded column from maximum score and represent end of common substring in sequence 2.

So the result of alignment between two score resulting of using coincidence substitution matrix is as follow, the common parts are bold:

Query:          **LMNCCH**

Sequence 2:     **LMNPA**

iii ) Scores and positions are returned to the CPU. So two sequences that have the longest common substring with query are determined depending on this scores.

The two sequences are preserved in text file with a developed format called tracer format as shown in the following.

Tracer format :

| |
|---|
| **SEQ1**<br>Q1,S1,L1<br>>sequence 1 name<br>**SEQ2**<br>Q2,S2,L2<br>>sequence 2 name<br>Sequence nucleotides or resudies<br>**QUERY**<br>Query nucleotides or resudies |

Q1 : position in query of the end of common substring between query and sequence 1.

S1: position in sequence 1 of end of common substring between query and sequence 1.

L1 : the length of common substring between query and sequence 1.

Q2 : position in query of the end of common substring between query and sequence 2.

S2: position in sequence 2 of end of common substring between query and sequence 2.

L2 : the length of common substring between query and sequence 2.

As the previous example :

Query = **LMNCCH** , Sequence 1 = **CCPKLM** , Sequence 2 =**LMNPA**

```
SEQ1
3,3,3
>Sequence 2
LMNPA
SEQ2
5,2,2
> Sequence 1
CCPKLM
QUERY
LMNCCH
```

***The third step,*** Text file that have the two sequences and query with alignment's score in tracer format is uploaded a web interface tool that is developed to show the common parts between query and each sequence in the same color, also shows the matching percentages of common substring length to the length of a query.

As the previous example :

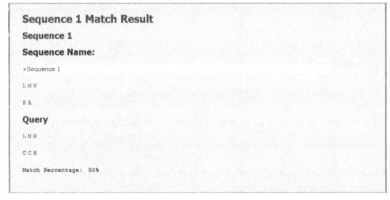

Figure 4.3 Common parts between Sequence 1 and Query.

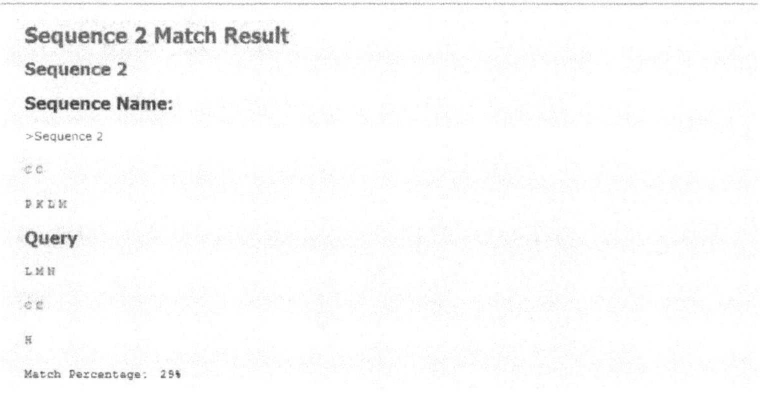

Figure 4.4 Common parts between Sequence 1 and Query.

## 4.2 Modifications of striemer's local alignment algorithm On GPU for GT-DB-GPU

An algorithm developed by M. Striemer [11] is used to get local alignment using GPU. As mentioned in chapter 2 it has some features such as i) It is 23 times faster than SSEARCH [21]. ii) It used BLOSUM 50 as substitution matrix. iii) query sequence and substitution matrix are stored in constant memory as hard coded because access to constant cache of GPU for reading is fast as access to register if all threads read the same address [27].

The following are proposed modifications to striemer's algorithm on GPU.

1 ) Striemer's algorithm is modified so that it finds protein or DNA sequence that has the highest alignment score instead of protein sequence only. 2) Striemer's algorithm is developed also to do function of gene tracer. After getting alignment score of each sequence in database, the highest 100 sequences score are extracted and saved in new database. Alignment scores of these 100 sequences with query are recomputed but using coincidence matrix and positions of scores in each sequence. Then two sequences with highest scores

are extracted and are preserved in text file and a developed web tool used to show the common substrings between sequences in text file in clear and difference color. 3) Another modifications is determining the suitable number of threads per block by calculating occupancy [27] instead of using just 64 thread as proposed by striemer's algorithm.

The following algorithm shows Gene Tracer algorithm with scanning database on GPU.

## 4.3 GT-DB-GPU algorithm

*Input :*

*Q_seq* : sequence //query protein or DNA sequence

*Output :*

*Seq_1 , Seq_2*: sequence // output sequences from database that have the
　　　　　　　　// longest common substrings with query .

*Variables :*

*Seq_score*: integer // matrix store score of each sequence

*Seq_DB_count*: integer // The number of sequence in database

*biological database* : database

*B_seq*: sequence // matrix to save 100 sequences that have highest score .

*i:* integer // matrix to preserve row number of score in computation matrix for
　　　// each sequence .

*j :* integer // matrix to preserve column number of score in matrix for each
　　　　　　// sequence .

*Seq_1* : sequence // sequence 1 from 100 sequences nearest to query .

*Seq_1_score* : integer // length of substring common between Q_seq , Seq_1

*Seq_2*: sequence // sequence 2 from 100 sequences nearest to query.

*Seq_2_score* : integer // length of substring common between Q_seq , Seq_2

*i_1* : integer // position of score in Q_seq for alignment between Q_seq& Seq_1

- 52 -

*j_1* : integer // position of score in Seq_1 for alignment between Q_seq& Seq_1

*i_2* :   integer  //   position  of  score  in  Q_seq  for  alignment  between
// Q_seq & /Seq_2

*j_2* : integer // position of score in Seq_2 for alignment between Q_seq& Seq_2

***Functions :***

*SW_GPU ( ) // Local alignment on GPU to compute score of alignment between*
*// query sequence and all sequences on database using*
*// Blosum50 substitution matrix .*

*SW_GT_GPU( ) // Local alignment  on GPU on 100 sequences and compute*
*//positions  of  scores  in  each  sequence  using  coincidence*
*// matrix .*

*Max (Seq_score ) // return the max100  sequences.*

*Max _GT(Seq_score ,row position matrix , column position matrix  ) // return*
*// the max 2 sequences scores with it's row and column positions .*

**Begin** :

// perform local alignment computations between query and sequences in
// database on GPU using BLOSUM50 substitution matrix .

Seq_score[Seq_DB_count] =

*SW_GPU*( Q_seq , BLOSUM50 **or** DNA_submatrix ,biological database)
// Get 100 sequence that have highest 100 score .
B_seq[100] = *Max*(Seq_score)

// perform SW computations between query sequence and 100 sequence saved
// in B_seq using coincidence  matrix .

( Seq_score[100] , i[100] , j[100] ) =
*SW_GT_GPU*( Q_seq , coincidence  matrix ,B_seq )
// Get the two sequences that have maximum score and also positions of score in
//each sequence ( j_1,j_2) , and in query ( i_1,i_2)

( Seq_1,Seq_1_score , i_1,j_1,Seq_2 , ,Seq_2_score,i_2,,j_2 )

$$= Max\_GT(\text{Seq\_score} , i , j)$$

**End**

## 4.3.1    SW sequence alignment on GPU function

*SW_GPU(*Q_seq , B_matrix , DB*)*

*{*

//Q_seq :query protein or DNA sequence

//B_matrix :   substitution matrix

//DB :   path to database

**Variables** :

Seq_count : integer //   count of sequences in DB

Seq_characters_length : integer // length of characters in each sequence .

Q_seq_characters_length : integer //   length of characters in Q_seq .

SW_matrix : integer //   computation matrix of SW

H : integer // score of current cell

temp_score   :   integer   //    keep   highest   score   during   computation   of

//  SW_matrix

score : integer //   matrix contains scores for all sequences

g   : integer // constant gap.

Sequence_DB : sequence // each sequence of database .

**Begin** :

// For each thread z ranging from 0 to Seq_count-1

k = 0

While ( k <Seq_count){

temp_score = 0

for (j=0;j< Seq_characters_length [z]) {

for (i=0;i<Q_seq_characters_lenght){

$north = H[i-1,j] - g$

$west = H[i,j-1] - g$

$north\_west = H[i-1,j-1] + B\_matrix\ (Q\_seq[i],Sequence\_DB[i])$

$H[i,j] := max\ (north, west, nort\_west, 0)$

SW_matrix[i][j] = H;

}

If ( H > temp_score ) Then temp_score = H ;

}

Score[k] = temp_score

k++

}

Return score // matrix contain scores for all sequences in DB

**End**


Time complexity of SW_GPU function is $O(m*n)$ and space complexity is ( $O(m*k)+O(k))$ where k is a sequence count in database, n length of query and m length of max sequence in database .

### 4.3.2    Gene tracer with proposed modifications

*SW_GT_GPU* (Q_seq , B_matrix , DB )

{

// Q_seq :query protein or DNA sequence

// B_matrix :  substitution matrix

// DB :   path to database

**Variables** :

Seq_count :  integer // count of sequences in DB.

Seq_characters_length : integer // length of characters in each sequence.

Q_seq_characters_length: integer // length of characters in Q_seq.

SW_matrix : integer //  computation matrix of SW.

H : integer // score of current cell.

temp_score : integer // keep highest score during computation of SW_matrix.

score : integer // matrix contain score for all sequences.

i_positions : integer // matrix to save positions of end of common sub in
//query for each sequence.

j_positions: integer // matrix to save positions of end of common sub in
// sequences.

**Begin** :

  // For each thread z

  k=0

  While ( k<Seq_count){

  temp_score= 0

  for (j=0 ; j<Seq_characters_length [z]) {

        for (i=0 ; i< Q_seq_characters_length){

    *north =H[i−1,j] − g*

    *west = H[i,j−1] − g*

    *north_west= H[i−1,j-1]+ B_matrix ( Q_seq[i],Sequence_DB[i])*

    *H[i,j] := max (north ,west,nort_west,0)*

        SW_matrix[i][j] = H;

        }

  If ( H > temp_score )

  {

    temp_score = H ;

    temp_i = i ;

    temp_j = j ;

  }

  }

  Score[k] = temp_score

  k++

i_positions [k]= i

j_positions[k] = j

}

Return score ,i_positions ,j_positions

**End**

Time complexity of SW_GT_GPU function is $O(m*n)$ and space complexity is $(O(m*100)+ 3*O(100 ))$ where n length of query and m length of maximum sequence length in database .

Then Time complexity of GT-DB-GPU algorithm is $O(m*n)$ and space complexity is ( $O(m*k)+O(k))$ where k is sequence count in database, n length of query and m length of max sequence in database .

## 4.4    Gene Tracer with scanning database using CPU vs GPU

The difference between GT-DB-CPU and GT-DB-GPU algorithms is that in GT-DB-GPU each thread of a GPU computes alignment between query and one sequence from database. So alignment of all sequences in database with query is computed in parallel. But in GT-DB-CPU, alignment of all sequences in database with query is computed serially. The difference is shown in the following.

### 4.4.1    GT-DB-CPU(3 nested loop)

For (z = 0 ; z < Sequence count in DB){

For ( j = 0 ; j < Sequence_DB _Length [z]){

For ( i=0 ; i < Query_length ){

Compute alignment for each cell

```
                              }
                          }
                      }
```

## 4.4.2    GT-DB-GPU ( 2 nested loop)

*// For each thread z*

Seq_DB _L = Sequence_DB _Length [z]

    For ( j = 0 ; j < Seq_DB _L){

        For ( i=0 ; i < Query_length ){

          Compute alignment for each cell

```
                              }
                      }
```

So GT-DB-CPU algorithm has total time complexity $O(m*n*z)$ and space complexity is ( $O(m*z) + 3*O(z)$ ) where n is the length of query, m is the length of maximum  sequence length in database and z is the sequences count in database.

## 4.5 Gene Tracer with scanning database on GPU Flow chart

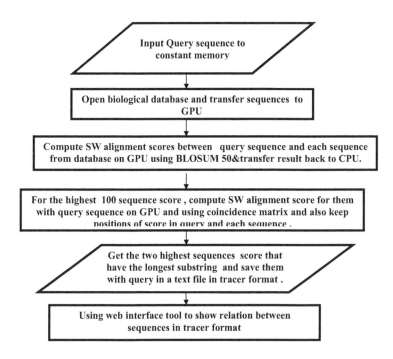

## 4.6 GT-DB-GPU algorithm outputs

The GT-DB-GPU algorithm was applied for both DNA sequences and proteins sequences with a query sequence , results obtained are as follow :

### 4.6.1 For proteins :

**Query input :**

MSFQNPSYINAKHRSFLQPKDTQDSQDLRNWVSHSSVDEETAYSSSTLS
SSSSKSFPCYDFEAAEMPETDVTITPQYVMDRVGKVADDRD

The text file contain results of alignment in tracer format is as shown in the following.

SEQ1
60,60,60
>sp|O74756|CHS2_SCHPO Chitin synthase-like protein 2
OS=Schizosaccharomyces pombe (strain 972 / ATCC 24843) GN=chs2
PE=2 SV=1
MSFQNPSYINAKHRSFLQPKDTQDSQDLRNWVSHSSVDEETAYSSST
LSSSSSKSFPCYDEYDEIKSPDDQKVEYMKTLRTLEEDAFSYTDSVY
DFEERSFDEHEPPIPPLHKTGVFSVPLQPTHTVNSNSDDGYENSSKNE
YLDFNSEISASPVNEPMTHSQSYTSIDRLNSSSSHYSKDVPLLCGSLTI
DCPTPIDLRGMLGPFMQKNPDEASFLRYSAITCQPDMNNNGLQLRT
WSTGRDIQIAVCLTLSDEDLASFAISLSSIMNNLKHLCSRSKSRVWGN
ESWEKVLVCVVIDGRNTVHQNVLDLLASIGVYQPHIAKGRVNGKRT
LSHMYEFTSTINVDEKLNLTTATGDGNV
SEQ2
90,450,30
>sp|B1YIA9|HSLU_EXIS2 ATP-dependent protease ATPase subunit HslU
OS=Exiguobacterium sibiricum (strain DSM 17290 / JCM 13490 / 255-15)
GN=hslU PE=3 SV=1
MHEFTPRQIVEKLNEHVIGQADAKRAVAIALRNRYRRQLLDPSLRDE
VTPKNILMIGPTGVGKTEIARRLAKLVRAPFVKIEATKFTEVGYVGR
DVESMVRDLVEASLRLVKDEKKEALKERAEAVANERIVDALVGKK
ASTGLGGGNPFEMLFGGTQKPPEQETANDTADRSVIRQQLFQGQLE
DRMIDVDIEERQMDLFSGQQGMEGLANLQDMLGQVMPKKTKKRQ
LSVKEARPILTAEEAERLLDLNEVHDEAVRRAEQMGIIFVDEIDKIAT
KGQDSAGVSREGVQRDILPIVEGSTVVTKYGPVKTDHMLFIAAGAF
HMAKPSDLIPELQGRFPIRVELDSLTEDDFVKILTEPNQALLKQYKAL
LGAEQVHVTFTEDAIRQIARIAAQVNDETDNIGARRLYTIMERVLEE
LSFEAAEMPETDVTITPQYVMDRVGKVADDRD
QUERY
MSFQNPSYINAKHRSFLQPKDTQDSQDLRNWVSHSSVDEETAYSSST
LSSSSSKSFPCYDFEAAEMPETDVTITPQYVMDRVGKVADDRD

- 60 -

This mean common substring between query and sequence 1 has length 60 and end in position 60 in sequence 1 and end in position 60 in query. Also common substring between query and sequence 2 has length 30 and end in position 450 in sequence 2 and end in position 90 in query.

Uploading text file of result :

## Sequence 1 Match Result

### Sequence 1

### Sequence Name:

>sp|O74756|CHS2_SCHPO Chitin synthase-like protein 2 OS=Schizosaccharomyces pombe (strain 972 / ATCC 24843) GN=chs2 PE=2 SV=1

MSFQNPSYINAKHRSFLQPKDTQDSQDLRNWVSHSSVDEETAYSSSTLSSSSSKSFPCYD

EYDEIKSPDDQKVEYMKTLRTLEEDAFSYTDSVYDFEERSFDEHEPPIPPLHKTGVFSVP

LQPTHTVNSNSDDGYENSSKNEYLDFNSEISASPVNEPMTHSQSYTSIDRLNSSSHYSK

DVPLLCGSLTIDCPTPIDLRGMLGPFMQKNPDEASFLRYSAITCQPEDMNNNGLQLRTWS

TGRDIQIAVCLTLSDEDLASFAISLSSIMNNLKHLCSRSKSRVWGNESWEKVLVCVVIDG

RNTVHQNVLDLLASIGVYQPHIAKGRVNGKRTLSHMYEFTSTINVDEKLNLTTATGDGNV

### Query

MSFQNPSYINAKHRSFLQPKDTQDSQDLRNWVSHSSVDEETAYSSSTLSSSSSKSFPCYD

FEAAEMPETDVTITPQYVMDRVGKVADDRD

Match Percentage:  67%

Figure 4.5 GT – DB - GPU's output for protein sequence 1 and offspring.

## Sequence 2 Match Result

### Sequence 2

### Sequence Name:

>sp|B1YIA9|HSLU_EXIS2 ATP-dependent protease ATPase subunit HslU OS=Exiguobacterium sibiricum (strain DSM 17290 / JCM 13490 / 255-15) GN=hslU PE=3 SV=1

MHEFTPRQIVEKLNEHVIGQADAKRAVAIALRNRYRRQLLDPSLRDEVTPKNILMIGPTG

VGKTEIARRLAKLVRAPFVKIEAIKFTEVGYVGRDVESMVRDLVEASLRLVKDEKKEALK

ERAEAVANERIVDALVGKKASTGLGGGNPFEMLFGGTQKPPEQETANDTADRSVIRQQLF

QGQLEDRMIDVDIEERQMDLFSGQQGMEGLAMLQDMLGQVMPKKTKKRQLSVKEARPILT

AEEAERLLDLNEVHDEAVRRAEQMGIIFVDEIDKIATKGQDSAGVSREGVQRDILPIVEG

STVVTKYGPVKTDHMLFIAAGAPHMAKPSDLIPELQGRFPIRVELDSLTEDDFVKILTEP

NQALLKQYKALLGAEQVHVTFTEDAIRQIARIAAQVNDETDNIGARRLYTIMERVLEELS

FEAAEMPETDVTITPQYVMDRVGKVADDRD

### Query

MSFQNPSYINAKHRSFLQPKDTQDSQDLRNWVSHSSVDEETAYSSTLSSSSSKSFPCYD

FEAAEMPETDVTITPQYVMDRVGKVADDRD

Match Percentage: 34%

Figure 4.6 GT – DB - GPU's output for protein sequence 2 and offspring .

As shown in figure 4.5 and figure 4.6 common parts between query & sequence 1 are in red color also matching percentage between query and sequence 1 are computed, where matching percentage equal to the length of common part divide by the length of query sequence .The same for sequence 2 with query.

## 4.6.2    For DNA :

Results of DNA Query sequence :

TTAGCAATCACTCGAAGTGTGCCAGGCCACGGCGCCCGGCCAGCAGT
GGGTTTTTATCTCCTTGTTTAGTGTTTATTCTCTTGT

Text result file :

SEQ1
25,60,25
>sp|Q0VFA3|GLD2_XENTR Poly(A) RNA polymerase GLD2
OS=Xenopus tropicalis
AAATAATTATCCTAACTAGTACCAAAGGCTTCCCCTTA
GCAATCACTCGAAGTGTGCCAGCACCTCCACTCACTTC
ACGTCAAGCGATTCCCATCATTGTTTCACTGATGGAGA
AACCAAGGCCCAGGGCACTTGGGGCAAGGCGTTCAGG
GGGCTTTCGGTCCGGAAGCAGCGTCGGGGCGGGAATT
CGAACCCTGGGTTCCCACACTGGCCCGTGGCAGGGCCC
CCAAGCCTTTTCCCAAACTGATCACAGAAAGTGACGAC
CCGTTCGCCCGGCGGACCGGGGGCGTCGGGCAGGTCCT
GGTCCAAGTGAGTGCCCGCCCCTGCCCTGGGCTGGCAG
AGTTCTTCCCCCAGCTGCAGGTAGACGTGGGAACCCGG
CAGGGTACGGAGCTGCTGGCGCGGCACGCTGATTAGA
AGCGGCGACTGCCCGTCAAGCATTCGCGCCTCTCCCCT
CCCTTGAGTTTCTTGGCAGGGT
SEQ2
85,247,50
>sp|B1YIA9|HSLU_EXIS2 ATP-dependent protease ATPase
subunit HslU
AGCGATCCTTCTGCCTCAGCCTCCCAAGTAGCTGGGAT
TACAGGCATGCGCCACCATGCCCAACTAATTTTTTTTGT
ACTTTTAGTAGAGACAGGGTTTCTCCACGTTGGTCAGG
CTGGTCTTGAACTCCTGACCTCAAGTGGTCTGCCTGCTT
CGGCCTCCCAAAGTGCTGGGATTACAGGCATGAGCCAC
GGCGCCCGGCCAGCAGTGGGTTTTTTATCTCCTTGTTTA
GTGTTTATTCTCTTGT
QUERY
TTAGCAATCACTCGAAGTGTGCCAGGCCACGGCGCCCG
GCCAGCAGTGGGTTTTTTATCTCCTTGTTTAGTGTTTAT
TCTCTTGT

This mean common substring between query and sequence 1 has length 25 and end in position 60 in sequence 1 and end in position 25 in query. Also common substring between query and sequence 2 has length 50 and end in position 247 in sequence 2 and end in position 85 in query .

Uploading text file of result :

## Sequence 1 Match Result

### Sequence 1

### Sequence Name:

>sp|Q0VFA3|GLD2_XENTR Poly(A) RNA polymerase GLD2 OS=Xenopus tropicalis
AAATAATTATCCTAACTAGTACCAAAGGCTTCCCC

TTAGCAATCACTCGAAGTGTGCCAG

CACCTCCACTCACTTCACGTCAAGCGATTCCCATCATTGTTTCACTGATGGAGAAACCAA

GGCCCAGGGCACTTGGGGCAAGGCGTTCAGGGGGCTTTCGGTCCGGAAGCAGCGTCGGGG

CGGGAATTCGAACCCTGGGTTCCCACACTGGCCCGTGGCAGGGCCCCCAAGCCTTTTCCC

AAACTGATCACAGAAAGTGACGACCCGTTCGCCCGGCGGACCGGGGGCGTCGGGCAGGTC

CTGGTCCAAGTGAGTGCCCGCCCCTGCCGTGGGCTGGCAGAGTTCTTCCCCCAGCTGCAG

GTAGACGTGGGAACCCGGCAGGGTACGGAGCTGCTGGCGCGGCACGCTGATTAGAAGCGG

CGACTGCCCGTCAAGCATTCGCGCCTCTCCCCTCCCTTGAGTTTCTTGGCAGGGT

### Query

TTAGCAATCACTCGAAGTGTGCCAG

GCCACGGCGCCCGGCCAGCAGTGGGTTTTTTATCTCCTTGTTTAGTGTTTATTCTCTTGT

Match Percentage: 30%

Figure 4.7 GT – DB - GPU's output for DNA  sequence 1 and offspring.

## Sequence 2 Match Result

### Sequence 2

### Sequence Name:

>sp|B1YIA9|HSLU_EXIS2 ATP-dependent protease ATPase subunit HslU
AGCGATCCTTCTGCCTCAGCCTCCCAAGTAGCTGGGATTACAGGCATGCGCCACCATGCC

CAACTAATTTTTTTTGTACTTTTAGTAGAGACAGGGTTTCTCCACGTTGGTCAGGCTGGT

CTTGAACTCCTGACCTCAAGTGGTCTGCCTGCTTCGGCCTCCCAAAGTGCTGGGATTACA

GGCATGAGCCACGGCGC

CCGGCCAGCAGTGGGTTTTTTATCTCCTTGTTTAGTGTTTATTCTCTTGT

### Query

TTAGCAATCACTCGAAGTGTGCCAGGCCACGGCGC

CCGGCCAGCAGTGGGTTTTTTATCTCCTTGTTTAGTGTTTATTCTCTTGT

Match Percentage: 59%

Figure 4.8 GT – DB - GPU's output for DNA  sequence 2 and offspring.

## 4.7    GT-DB-GPU's execution time on GPU vs CPU

GT-DB-GPU algorithm was implemented on a GPU Tesla C2075 . It has total memory 6 GByte and 448 CUDA cores. Each core is 1.15 GHZ. The algorithm was implemented using CUDA C extension in Microsoft visual studio environment. GPU execution time is measured and compared with execution time on CPU using device with core i3 multiprocessor each core is 2.27 GHZ. Main memory is 4 GByte and run windows 7 - 64 bit. The tested biological database contains 300,000 sequence.

Results of execution time on GPU vs CPU are as shown in table 4.5 .

Table 4-6 Execution time of gene tracer on GPU and CPU using 64 thread per block.

| Query sequence Length | GPU time(Sec) | CPU time(Sec) | Speed up ratio |
|---|---|---|---|
| 8 | 1.5 | 120 | 80 |
| 16 | 3 | 240 | 80 |
| 32 | 6 | 540 | 90 |
| 64 | 13 | 1050 | 80.7 |
| 128 | 24 | 2820 | 117.5 |
| 256 | 47 | 6570 | 140 |
| 512 | 97.5 | 10800 | 111 |
| 768 | 145.5 | 17400 | 119.5 |
| 1024 | 189 | 23040 | 118 |

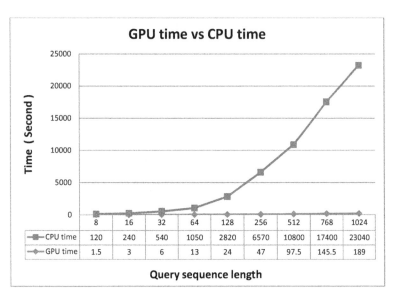

Figure 4.9 GPU vs CPU execution time for GT-DB-GPU.

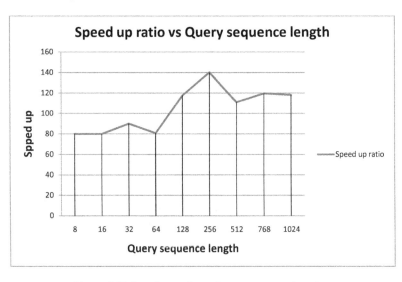

Figure 4.10 Speed up ratio vs Query sequence length.

These results show that implementation of algorithm on GPU is 140 faster than execution on CPU due to parallel execution of algorithm on a GPU where each thread computes alignment between query and a sequence in database. CPU computes alignment between query and each sequence in database serially.

## 4.8 Effect of number of threads per block on execution time

In this section effect of the number of threads per block on occupancy and so execution time will be discussed. The number of threads is determined depending on calculating occupancy and then it's effect on execution time. This is one of main contributions in thesis.

To optimize execution of programs on GPU, multiprocessors on the device should be kept busy. So it is very important to design applications by using threads and blocks in a way that maximizes hardware usage. Threads of blocks are divided into warps and each multiprocessor executes some of this warps. As the number of warps increases per multiprocessor, multiprocessors will be more busy because if a warp is paused or stalled then another warp is executed and this decreases latencies and keeps hardware as busy as possible. A metric that is used to measure utilization of hardware called occupancy and is a key measure for GPU efficiency[37]. Occupancy is the ratio of the number of active warps per multiprocessor to the maximum number of possible active warps per multiprocessor.

Limitation factors for occupancy are 1) the number of active threads per block. 2) The number of registers used in the kernel. 3) The amount of shared memory allocated for block in the kernel. Equations that are used to determine occupancy is shown in the following [27].

## 4.8.1    GPU's Occupancy computing equations

$$Occupancy = \frac{Active\ Warps\ per\ Multiprocessor}{Warps\ per\ multiprocessor} * 100$$

Active Warps per Multiprocessor = A_Th_MP * No_W_B

- No_W_B : Number of warps per block.

$$No\_W\_B = ceil(\frac{Number\ of\ threads}{Warp\ size}, 1),$$

Warp size $= 32$, As defined by Nvidia [27]

- A_Th_MP : Number of active thread blocks per multiprocessor

  A_Th_MP= Minumum ( A1, A2,A3)

- A1 : The maximum number of thread blocks per multiprocessor limited by maximum blocks per multiprocessor (physical limit ) .

$A1 = 8$ , As defined by Nvidia [27]

- A2 : The maximum number of thread blocks per multiprocessor limited by registers per multiprocessor .

$$A2 = \frac{Maximum\ number\ of\ registers\ per\ multiprocessor}{Number\ of\ registers\ allocatable\ to\ block\ (Rblock)}$$

For devices with compute capability 2.0 :

$$Rblock = ceil(\ number\ of\ register\ for\ thread * Warp\ size, 64\ ) * No\_W\_B$$

- A3 : The maximum number of thread blocks per multiprocessor limited by shared memory per multiprocessor.

$$A3 = \frac{\textbf{Shared memory per Multiprocessor}}{\textbf{Sblock}}$$

For devices with compute capability 2.0 :

$$Sblock = ceil\ (Sk, 128)$$

Occupancy calculator spreadsheet on excel was designed depending on these equations by Nvidia to measure occupancy. Occupancy 100 % is the best utilization of hardware. The best value of the number of threads per block is determined so that give occupancy 100 %.

Striemer's algorithm [11] assumes number of threads per block 64. The number of registers used is 13. The shared memory per block is 1152 Byte.

In occupancy calculator , occupancy was measured using these values and found to be 33 %, result is as shown in figure 4.11. This mean the number of active warps to multiprocessor is 33 % of maximum number of warps per multiprocessor, so this number of threads was not acceptable. As shown in figure 4.11 there are 3 sections. Section 1, determine the compute capability of GPU device used and shared memory size per multiprocessor.

| | |
|---|---|
| 1.) Select Compute Capability (click): | 2.0 |
| 1.b) Select Shared Memory Size Config (bytes) | 49152 |
| | |
| 2.) Enter your resource usage: | |
| Threads Per Block | 64 |
| Registers Per Thread | 13 |
| Shared Memory Per Block (bytes) | 1152 |

(Don't edit anything below this line)

| 3.) GPU Occupancy Data is displayed here and in the graphs: | |
|---|---|
| Active Threads per Multiprocessor | 512 |
| Active Warps per Multiprocessor | 16 |
| Active Thread Blocks per Multiprocessor | 8 |
| Occupancy of each Multiprocessor | 33% |

| Physical Limits for GPU Compute Capability: | 2.0 |
|---|---|
| Threads per Warp | 32 |
| Warps per Multiprocessor | 48 |
| Threads per Multiprocessor | 1536 |
| Thread Blocks per Multiprocessor | 8 |
| Total # of 32-bit registers per Multiprocessor | 32768 |
| Register allocation unit size | 64 |
| Register allocation granularity | warp |
| Registers per Thread | 63 |
| Shared Memory per Multiprocessor (bytes) | 49152 |
| Shared Memory Allocation unit size | 128 |
| Warp allocation granularity | 2 |
| Maximum Thread Block Size | 1024 |

Figure 4.11 Occupancy calculator result of 64 thread.

Section 2, limitation factors on occupancy are fed. Section 3, GPU occupancy data is computed and displayed such as active warps per multiprocessor, active threads per multiprocessor and occupancy. Occupancy is 33 %. The last section includes physical limits for GPU that are constant for device such as warps per multiprocessor is the maximum number of warps allocated to multiprocessor.

Effect of changing number of threads per block on occupancy.

Number of threads per block is increased by 32 value and computing occupancy and execution time[27]. So at number of threads is 96 thread and occupancy will be 50 % and execution time is 185 at a query length 1024 . Therefore when occupancy decreases, execution time decreased also. Number of threads is increased by 32 due to warp size is 32[27].

Number of threads is increased by 32 and measure occupancy until it reach 100 % at 192 thread. By calculating execution time at 192 thread, it's 172 second . That is as shown in table 4.7.

Table 4-7 GPU's occupancy vs # of threads.

| # of threads | Occupancy | Execution Time (Sec) |
|:---:|:---:|:---:|
| 64 | 33 % | 189 |
| 96 | 50% | 185 |
| 128 | 67% | 177 |
| 160 | 83% | 174 |
| 192 | 100% | 172 |

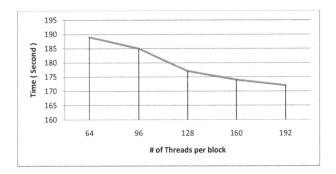

Figure 4.12  GT-DB - GPU time vs # of threads per block

As shown in table 4.7, there are small max difference in execution time (~ 17 sec ). But this show effect of occupancy on execution time. So determining the suitable number of threads per block is very important. In some applications increasing occupancy may not improve performance [27], so measuring occupancy and execution time correspond to it, and then the number of threads that give minimum execution time is determined. In the following are steps to determine suitable number of threads for application.

### 4.8.2 Steps to determine the suitable number of threads per block

1- Assume suitable initial number threads.

2- Calculate shared memory per block (as mention in occupancy equations ) and using occupancy calculator to determine occupancy.

3- If occupancy less than 100 %, increase number of threads per block by 32.

4- Measure occupancy and execution time and repeat step 3 if occupancy less than 100 % until it reach 100%.

5- Choose the number of thread give minimum execution time that in many cases at occupancy 100 % but in some cases increasing occupancy don't improve performance.

# Chapter 5: Conclusion and Future work

Three main contributions are proposed in this thesis. i) Gene Tracer algorithm was developed based on pairwise local alignment algorithm and is used to determine and locate common parts between DNA or Protein sequence (offspring) and other two DNA or Protein sequences (ancestors) and also computes percentage of contributions of ancestors sequences in offspring sequence. ii) Gene Tracer algorithm was extended, so it determines origins of a sequence by scanning database on GPU. This extended algorithm was abbreviated GT - DB - GPU. The main application of GT -DB -GPU algorithm is extracting ancestors sequences of an offspring sequence from biological database using GPU and then locates common parts between offspring and each one of the two ancestors. Algorithm's implementation on GPU has maximum speed up 140 times than implementation on CPU. iii) More reduction in execution time on GPU was reached by increasing occupancy to 100 %. It was found that the number of threads per block increases so occupancy increases. For query sequence having a length 1024, database contains 300000 sequences, the number of thread was 64 per block, so occupancy was 33 % and execution time was 189 second on GPU. For the same query sequence and database increasing the number of thread to 192 per block, occupancy was 100 % and execution time was 172 second on GPU. There was 9 % reduction in time. Steps of determining suitable number of threads per block were listed.

To the above contributions, an important point is the limitations of GPU usage. GPU's cost and Developing software for GPU are the two important limitations for GPU usage. GPU's cost is added to total cost of a PC.

The GPU device that was used in testing and gave significant optimization is more expensive than CPU. Developing software for GPUs is more complex than doing the same for CPU code. It is not easy to recommend the use of GPU for all applications due to its cost and development of its software. But if one must have better performance for applications, then GPUs might be an attractive option.

For future work, I suggest development of the GT - DB – GPU algorithm so that it can deal with many offsprings at the same time and extracted the ancestors for each offspring sequence that has certain properties. Also I suggest using cloud computing system as an environment of execution and its usage is compared to GPU.

# References

[1] A. W.Liew , H.Yan and M.Yang, "Pattern recognition techniques for the emerging field of bioinformatics : A review ", the journal of Pattern Recognition society , October 2006 .

[2] Mourad Elloumi, Albert Y. Zomaya," Algorithms in Computational Molecular Biology: Techniques, Approaches" and Applications edited , , 2011, John Wiley & Sons .

[3] W.pearson, D.lipman , "Improved tools for biological sequence comparison", Proc. Nat.Acad. Sci. USA , Vol. 85, pp. 2444-2448, April 1988 .

[4] J. SETUBAL , J. MEIDANIS ," introduction of computational molecular biology " , PWS PUBLISHING 1997.

[5] K.R. Sharma , "Bioinformatics Sequence Alignment and Markov Models", McGraw-Hill 2009.

[6] J. C. Venter, M. D. Adams, E. W. Myers, et al., "The sequence of the human genome," Science 291 (2001), 1304–1351 .

[7] W. Liu, B. Schmidt, G. Voss, A. Schroder, and W. Muller-Wittig, " Bio-Sequence Database Scanning on a GPU ", in Proc. 20th IEEE International Parallel & Distributed Processing Symposium (IPDPS'06), 5th IEEE International Workshop on High Performance Computational Biology) Workshop (HICOMB'06), Rhode Island, Greece : (2006).

[8] T. F. Smith, M. S. Waterman, "Identification of common molecular subsequences", J. Molecular Biology, no. 147, pp. 195-197, 1981.

[9] C. S. B Needleman, C. D. Wunsch, "A general method applicable to the search for similarities in the amino acid sequence of two proteins". Journal of molecular biology, vol. 48, no. 1, pp. 443-453. 1970.

[10] S.Coull, B.Szymanski , "Sequence alignment for masquerade detection", Computational Statistics and Data Analysis 52 (2008) 4116–4131

[11] Gregory M. Striemer and Ali Akoglu ," Sequence Alignment with GPU: Performance and Design Challenges", IEEE Xplore,2009

[12] T.Cormen , E.Rivest and C.Stelin ,"introduction to algorithms ", The MIT Press Cambridge, Massachusetts London, England .

[13] M. O. Dayhoff, R. M. Schwartz, B. C. Orcutt," A model of evolutionary change in proteins, in Atlas of Protein Sequence and Structure", chapter 22, National Biomedical Research Foundation, Washington, DC: (1978), p345–358.

[14] S. Henikoff, J. G. Henikoff, "Amino acid substitution matrices from protein blocks", Proc. Natl. Acad. Sci. USA, Vol. 89, N°22: (1992), p10915-10919.

[15] M . Elloumi , Y. Zomaya , " Algorithms in Computational Molecular Biology: Techniques, Approaches and Applications " , 2011, John Wiley & Sons .

[16] X. Huang, K. M. Chao, "A generalized global Alignment algorithm, Bioinformatics", Vol. 19, N°2: (2003), p228–233.

[17 ] http://www.seas.gwu.edu/~simhaweb/cs151/lectures/module12/align.html .

[18] D.Hirschberg. "A linear space algorithm for computing maximal common sub expressions". Communications ofthe ACM, 18(6)

[19] W.pearson, D.lipman , "Improved tools for biological sequence comparison", Proc. Nat.Acad. Sci. USA , Vol. 85, pp. 2444-2448, April 1988 .

[20] S.Altschul , W.Gish, W.Miller, E.Myers , and D. Lipman. "Basic local alignment search tool". Journal of Molecular Biology, 1990

[21] W. R. Pearson, "Searching protein sequence libraries: Comparison of the sensitivity and selectivity of the Smith-Waterman and FASTA algorithms,"Genomics, vol. 11, no. 3, pp. 635–650, Nov. 1991 .

[22] A. M.Hosny , H. A Shedeed , A. S. Hussein and M. F. Tolba "An Efficient Solution for Aligning Huge DNA Sequences" , International Journal of Computer Applications ,Vol 32 , October 2011 .

[23] S. Sarkar, T. Majumder, A. Kalyanaraman, "Hardware Accelerators for Biocomputing: A Survey" , IEEE Explorer , 2010 .

[24] M. Farrar, " Striped Smith-Waterman speeds database searches six times over other SIMD implementations", Bioinformatics, Vol. 23, Issue 2 : (2007), p156-161.

[25] Rognes Torbjørn, "Faster Smith-Waterman database searches with inter-sequence SIMD parallelisation," BMC Bioinformatics, vol. 12, no. 1, p. 221, 2011.

[26] P . Zhang, N. Sun, X. Jiang, X. Liu. L. Xu, "A reconfigurable accelerator for smith-waterman algorithm," Circuits and Systems II: Express Briefs, IEEE Transactions on, vol. 54, no. 12, pp. 1077 - 1081 , December 2007.

[27] Nvidia Programming Guide   http://developer.Nvidia.com/Nvidia-gpu-programming-guide .

[28] J. Krüger and R. Westermann, Linear algebra operators for GPU implementation of numerical algorithms, ACM Transactions on Graphics (TOG), in Proc ACM SIGGRAPH'03, Vol. 22, Issue 3 : (July 2003), p908–916.

[29] P. Agarwal, S. Krishnan, N. Mustafa, and S. Venkatasubramanian. Streaming geometric optimization using graphics hardware, in Proc. 11th Annual European Symposium on Algorithms (ESA'03), Budapest, Hungary : (September, 2003).

[30] M. Charalambous, P. Trancoso, and A. Stamatakis. Initial experiences porting a bioinformatics application to a graphics processor, in Proc. 10th Panhellenic Conference on Informatics (PCI'05), Volos, Greece : (November 2005).

[31] D. Shreiner, M. Woo, J. Neider, and T. Davis, " OpenGL Programming Guide", 5th ed. Reading, MA: Addison-Wesley, Aug. 2005.

[32] Nvidia CUDA parallel programming (http://www.Nvidia.com/object/cuda_home_new.html)

[33] Y. Liu, W. Huang, J. Johnson, S. Vaidya, " GPU accelerated Smith-Waterman ", in Proc. Computational Science (ICCS'06), Lecture Notes in Computer Science, Vol. 3994, Springer-Verlag, Berlin, Germany : (2006), p188-195.

[34] S. A. Manavski and G. Valle, "CUDA compatible GPU cards as efficient hardware accelerators for Smith-Waterman sequence alignment", *BMC Bioinformatics,* Vol. 9 (Suppl 2), S10 : (2008).

[35] Yuma Munekawa, Fumihiko Ino , Kenichi Hagihara , "Design and implementation of the Smith-Waterman Algorithm on the CUDA-Compatible GPU" , 2008 .

[36] http://alg.csie.ncnu.edu.tw/DataSet/BLOSUM%2050.txt.

[37] http://docs.nvidia.com/cuda/cuda-c-best-practices-guide/index.html.

www.ingramcontent.com/pod-product-compliance
Lightning Source LLC
LaVergne TN
LVHW092343060326

832902LV00008B/781